Meet Click Millionaires!

With online lifestyle businesses that allow them to enjoy life more while working less, these Click Millionaires will never go back to corporate life!

Kristin—who makes a fun living blogging from a beautiful vineyard in the south of France (Chapter 10).

Dave—who turned his passion for remote-control airplanes into a profitable career as one of YouTube's most popular stars (Chapter 12).

Al—who uses industry expertise from his previous job to publish an email newsletter that's more popular than his former employer's (Chapter 9).

Giancarlo—who founded an easy-to-start online business with no products of his own, before he even graduated from college (Chapter 15).

Khrystyne—who left the corporate world behind to take her pick of clients and projects as a flexible freelancer (Chapter 17).

Rob—whose surprising hobby helped him quit his job and build a profitable online community for over 100,000 friends (Chapter 13).

Ann—whose multilevel marketing success online has helped her husband and son quit their jobs to work with her from home (Chapter 16).

The **three brothers** from Germany who have become billionaires by simply imitating hot U.S. start-up ideas for themselves (Chapter 18).

And many, many more inspiring examples of Click Millionaire lifestyle business success!

click millionaires

work less, live more with an internet business you love

SCOTT C. FOX

AMACOM AMERICAN MANAGEMENT ASSOCIATION
New York ▸ Atlanta ▸ Brussels ▸ Chicago ▸ Mexico City
San Francisco ▸ Shanghai ▸ Tokyo ▸ Toronto ▸ Washington, D.C.

The author, ClickMillionaires.com, ScottFox.com, The Liminal Success Institute, or associated websites, services, persons, or entities may have content, promotional, advertising, customer, consulting, or equity relationships with the people or companies discussed or recommended in this book and on associated websites. Many of the links included in this book and on associated websites contain affiliate advertising codes. While efforts have been made to identify the best suppliers/vendors in each of these areas, we accept no liability for your use of them. You should use your own independent judgment and/or professional advice to evaluate their services and fit for your needs. Nothing herein should be construed as any guarantee of financial success for readers and any representations or inferences of financial success by readers are specifically disclaimed. The tools, strategies, and examples in this and related materials and services are not necessarily representative of the average person's success. No representation is made as to the completeness or accuracy of these contents. All marks belong to their respective owners. The author, publisher, and all related entities specifically disclaim any liability, loss, or risk that is incurred as a consequence, directly or indirectly, of the use and application of any of the contents of this or related works, websites, or products.

Library of Congress Cataloging-in-Publication Data

Fox, Scott C.
Click millionaires : work less, live more with an internet business you love / Scott C. Fox. — 1st ed.
    p. cm.
Includes bibliographical references and index.
ISBN 978-0-8144-3191-7 — ISBN 0-8144-3191-7 1. Electronic commerce. 2. Small business—Management. I. Title.
HF5548.32.F69 2012
658.8'72—dc23

2012004882

Printing number
10 9 8 7 6 5 4 3

To my dad, who dedicated his life and career to helping others, and inspired me to do the same.

CONTENTS

. . . .

introduction
work doesn't have to be
something you hate

HOW ARE YOU going to feel come Monday morning? When that
alarm clock goes off, are your eyes going to snap open and sparkle
with enthusiasm? Are you going to head off to your commute with a
spring in your step? Are you looking forward to weeks, months, and
years of that routine?

I really hope you are, but sadly the odds are against it. In fact,
according to one study, almost 60 percent of people around the world
don't like their jobs![1] And the Conference Board recently recorded
the highest level of job unhappiness among American workers in its
20-plus-year history of doing similar surveys.[1]

You probably work too much for too little with people you don't like doing stuff you don't care much about. At least part of that sounds like you, right? I don't think it's healthy to spend all your waking hours working a job you don't like just so you can get up to do it again tomorrow. And then to keep doing it forever hoping to save enough so that you can eventually quit and then do *nothing*.

Most self-help books focus on changing your attitude, envisioning abundance, or fixing your relationships. But the real problem is that most people hate their jobs and don't have enough money. Most of us spend more time at work than anywhere else. If you spend any of your after-hours time watching TV, sleeping, or commuting, that leaves just a couple of daily hours where your kids, spouse, friends, hobbies, church, and everything else get any time at all.

So the real issue is *your work*. Do you love your work? Do you spend your days doing work you feel you were born to do? Or do you at least get paid enough to make all the frustrating daily compromises more than worth it?

If you're reading this book, I'm betting the answer is no.

You're here because it's your career that needs fixing. It's the 8 to 10 to 14 hours each day you waste just trying to cover your bills and get ahead a little. You can pursue the Law of Attraction to "manifest abundance in your life" all you want, but if you're working a 9-to-5 (or an 8-to-8) job that leaves you unfulfilled, it's time for a change! *Your job should help you live the life you want, not force you into a lifestyle you don't enjoy just to keep your bills paid.* Instead, how about building a lifestyle you like today so you don't have to postpone so much of your life until retirement?

Join the Click Millionaires Revolution!

This book shares details of the unprecedented opportunity you have to (re)design your career and life to achieve financial independence and success on your own terms. It can help you leave behind many of the compromises and frustrations that plague corporate life and start the transition from making your boss rich to enriching your own life instead.

While the media and many business books assume you need to be a software geek or a Stanford MBA to "succeed" online, I believe you already have the credentials you need to build a profitable *Internet lifestyle business* based on your own real-life experience and interests.

I know all this sounds suspiciously "get rich quick" but it's not. Through lots of hard work and clever use of the Internet, I have found this lifestyle and financial success myself and I wrote this book to help you find it, too. Like my earlier books, *Internet Riches* and *e-Riches 2.0*, this book is filled with specific proven strategies and tools that I have used personally to build a more prosperous and flexible future.

Here's the plan for sharing them with you:

Part One: Identify your top lifestyle goals so you can design them into a new online business.

Part Two: Discover the revolutionary principles behind the success of Click Millionaire lifestyle businesses so that you can use them to make money yourself. Plus, learn how to quickly position yourself as an expert in any field online.

Parts Three and Four: Read inspiring real-life case studies of successful online entrepreneurs who are living the "Click Millionaires Lifestyle." Many of these lifestyle entrepreneurs have created profitable new products and services of their own, while others have built successful online businesses by providing promotional or freelance services to others.

Part Five: Pinpoint a profitable niche business model of your own that takes advantage of your personal life experience and interests to make money online.

Part Six: Learn the easiest, fastest, and cheapest ways to build websites and collect money from your new customers online.

Part Seven: Create an Action Plan for implementing Click Millionaire lifestyle design strategies and choosing the right niche business model in your own life so you can get started on the work you were born to do.

Why Should You Listen to Me?

I grew up on the lower end of middle-class in dangerous and poor inner-city Detroit, but managed to make myself a millionaire. I worked my way up with no inside connections or family money, paying my own way through both the University of Michigan and Stanford Law School. I earned my first small fortune on Wall Street and retired for the first time when I was just 25. After I got bored scuba diving in the islands of the South Pacific, I worked my way to success again in Silicon Valley and then again in Hollywood, too, building expertise at starting highly profitable, cutting-edge Internet businesses.

Now that I am able to spend my time how I want, I want to help you succeed, too. This book is full of my personal stories and recommendations so I apologize if it sounds like I'm trying to impress you or sell you. These personal examples are the best way I know to share with you my enthusiasm and the benefits of the many lessons I've learned earning my own success online. I want you to know that I don't write my books hoping to make money from you by writing about success I've never had myself. I've literally traveled the world to identify the best lifestyle and business opportunities available today. I'm an active entrepreneur, strategy consultant, and investor making money from a dozen different website businesses as you read this. And I donate my book profits to charity to "pay it forward" helping others to succeed like I have.

I have a popular YouTube channel (www.youtube.com/scottfox1), Twitter account (www.twitter.com/scott_fox), Google+ (www.scottfoxongoogle.com) and Facebook pages (www.facebook.com/click-millionaire), my Click Millionaires Radio Show podcasts (www.Click MillionairesRadio.com) and all the other tools online to prove to you that I know what I'm talking about. Why? Because I want you to know that I do this stuff myself—I don't just write about it.

And you know what? It works!

The best of these resources is ClickMillionaires.com. That's where we're building the friendliest and most helpful community online for people like you who want to build their own lifestyle businesses. It's where you'll find my best blog posts, podcasts, and latest videos, plus free updates to this book, and where you'll get to meet other Click Millionaires from around the world, too. Please come join the community to become part of our worldwide movement toward redefining success for ourselves by building ethical, fulfilling lifestyle businesses online and helping others do it, too.

The New American Dream for You

Today you can do better than trying to work your way up to the *corner office*. Building a successful business in your *home office* can let you enjoy your work more, worry less about money, spend more time with family, work on projects you enjoy, and share that success with others, too.

Reading this book isn't suddenly going to make you $1,000,000. But reading it will give you the tools to redesign your career and life like I have. I hope that you enjoy it and that it's helpful to you in creating a life you are happier to live.

I would love your feedback, suggestions, and follow-up questions. What would you like to hear more about? What tips, tricks, tools, and tactics do you have more questions about? Where do you want to go next now that you have this new info? How can I help you succeed? Visit me online so we can work together to help you work less, live more, and build a meaningful, profitable life that you can be proud of.

Welcome to the world of Click Millionaires.

Scott Fox

Open only to my readers: ClickMillionaires.com is the online marketing and e-commerce startup coaching community I've built just for you. It continues the experience and friendly education you started by buying this book. Visit ClickMillionairesReader.com and answer the secret questions to gain access—as a reader of this book your membership at ClickMillionaires.com is free. You don't even need to have a website to participate!

INTRODUCTION NOTES
1. jobs.aol.com/articles/2011/03/04/most-business-professionals-are-unhappily-employed/
2. www.conference-board.org/publications/publicationdetail.cfm?publicationid=1727; The Conference Board, John M. Gibbons, January 2010, Report Number: R-1459-09-RR

PART ONE

REDESIGNING YOUR LIFESTYLE FOR SUCCESS

· · · · · · 1 · · · · · ·

work less, live more
becoming a click millionaire

The trouble with the rat race is that even if you win, you're still a rat.
—Lily Tomlin, actress and comedian

THERE HAS TO BE a better way!

Isn't that what you have been thinking? Are you tired of the work you do, or the people you work with, or the low pay or uncertain career path? Or maybe all of the above? Or the fact that you may have to continue that same routine for years or decades more? Do you really think that you're going to be able to save your way to a comfortable retirement working for someone else? Aren't the odds of a comfortable retirement small unless you save so much that your working years are painfully light on luxuries, vacations, and toys?

If you are like I used to be, you probably thought getting that corporate job was a ticket to both money and security. Unfortunately corporate employment has turned out to be more of an "income for dummies" plan than a lifetime meal ticket. You are still required to contribute most of your waking hours to the corporate bottom line—but that's no longer a guarantee for steady pay, job security, decent health coverage, and a comfortable retirement. Sadly, the only person who cares about your personal fulfillment and financial independence is you. Add the daily pressure of commuting to an office, working with people you normally wouldn't spend time with, pursuing priorities set by people who don't understand the needs of your customers, plus the constant threat of layoffs, it's no wonder that more and more people feel trapped in a rat race from which they can't escape!

Don't Just Get a Job, Get a Life

If you challenge traditional assumptions about career priorities, you can discover that there are new solutions to these work-life balance issues. It's okay to put your own life ahead of making money or climbing the corporate ladder and you don't have to do work you dread just to keep afloat. Today you have the opportunity to redesign your life around what's important to *you* and *define success for yourself*. You can choose to build a *lifestyle business online* that supports both your family and your own personal life goals, even with little capital or technical training.

Redefining success on your own terms can allow you to rebalance your life to achieve the goals most important to you. Instead of focusing simply on making money, I'd like to help you find the courage to define your success not just in dollars, fancy cars, or shiny objects that are promoted to you on television, but to include increased flex-ibility, creativity, and happiness, too. But motivation and a willing-ness to make some sacrifices along the way are not all you need to build a profitable lifestyle business for yourself. You need specific practical recommendations about which online business opportuni-ties and tools are the best today. Personalizing those recommenda-tions into a plan that you act upon can make the difference between *wishing* you were successful and *being* successful.

I wrote this book to help you do just that.

This Book Is Different

Too much online moneymaking advice is focused on finding clever but unsustainable ways to attract more website traffic. That kind of approach focuses on tricks—it helps you exploit small advantages in pay-per-click (PPC) advertising or search engine optimization (SEO), or attracting traffic from the latest YouTube, Twitter, Facebook, Google+, app, plug-in, software, or other "hacks."

These approaches sometimes work, but by the time an online marketing "guru" gets around to telling (and selling) you his latest traffic-attraction tricks, you can be sure that there's not much money left in that competitive market.

More importantly, *building businesses on temporary market inefficien-cies doesn't build the long-term asset value and recurring income of the Click Millionaire business system that I want for you.*

So, this book is not going to teach you how to become the 100,000th person to rehash diet secrets into a free e-book, build a huge email list overnight with YouTube videos or mobile apps, or use Google Adwords PPC ads to promote affiliate marketing offers.

Instead of teaching you to push a product that may be outdated in six months and require you to start over again, this book is going to help you develop a new business and career that grows into a satisfying ongoing *lifestyle* for you. It's going to teach you to redefine success for yourself, redesign your life around the things that matter most to you, and support that lifestyle with your own Internet-based business that allows you to enjoy the financial independence, creative control, and schedule flexibility traditionally only available to people who already had millions in the bank.

The goal is to find a *lifestyle balance* that is comfortable and fulfilling for you.

You Can Build a Business as Unique as You Are

My goal for you is to create something *new;* an original and unique business that positions you as an expert in your chosen field; a business that channels your efforts into something more significant than just increasing your click-through rate by 0.01 percent; a business that targets niche needs that speak to you and those in your target market on a fundamental level. I'd like to help you mine your niche to generate long-term recurring profits from a sustainable, personally satisfying lifestyle business that is meaningful to you.

For example:

- How about building a business around your unique personal experience so that you can help others solve similar problems in their own lives?

- Or developing an interest you have into a new expertise you can use to help advise others with similar interests?

- And delivering that information or those products in a cost-effective, consistent, ethical way that attracts loyal customers to create a profitable business around you and your favorite hobbies?

I have done this personally in a bunch of market spaces that most "experts" and keyword research would have said were saturated, including probably the most competitive area of all, Internet marketing. Together we'll make sure that your approach will be different, successful, and practical, too.

What's a "Lifestyle Business"?

A lifestyle business is one where you prioritize lifestyle benefits over growth and profits.

It's a real business that makes you real money but one that also lets you enjoy more of the life you deserve. With little risk or cash investment, these new kinds of online businesses can help you create a "laptop lifestyle" that finally frees you from working for someone else. Plus, they can make you happier because you spend your time working on projects you choose with people you like. The money is not the point. Your lifestyle as the owner is.

You may feel like you're not qualified to build your own business, or that the niches that interest you must be "wrong" because they don't fit traditional MBA approaches. But business schools (and most business books) teach people how to work for and grow corporations, not build happier lives. With lifestyle businesses the emphasis is on your lifestyle at least as much as on the business. This means that (unlike with corporate jobs or business school management theories) you can prioritize your own lifestyle interests first and even have multiple business lines at the same time. And who's more of an expert on what you want out of life than you?

Business school professors, economists, and bankers turn up their noses at this kind of business, because it doesn't require venture capital and isn't aimed at maximizing profits, increasing shareholder value, or issuing an IPO. But I *love* those businesses.

Let's face it, you're not on track to become a billionaire anyway. Wouldn't you be happy with a six-figure business that was in a field you like, with low costs, few politics or management challenges, and that allowed you to control your own schedule? (Especially if that business had the potential to grow even more profitable through free Internet distribution and automated online marketing?)

Sorry, business school professors: your traditional corporate definitions of success don't apply to Click Millionaire lifestyle businesses.

The goal of most big companies seems to be growth for growth's sake. And the most ambitious people used to want to work for those big companies. But today the pressure of big company jobs has many professionals I know wishing for something less stressful, *even if it means taking a cut in pay.*

"Big" also used to be a requirement for business because it took lots of people to do stuff. People needed to explain product features and make sales, people needed to process paperwork, people needed to check inventory and coordinate with suppliers, people needed to spread the word through advertising and marketing, and so forth. But the Net has changed all that. Decades of competition in the software industry have created powerful Internet-based systems for publishing, distribution, and marketing that any start-up or small business owner can use for just a few dollars/month. Today most order-taking and sales functions can be automated through a simple website shopping cart that will track your inventory, too. A lot of marketing can get done even while you're at the beach or asleep— your website doesn't go to the beach and your online ads keep running while you're sleeping!

All this means that the "small" in small business no longer means small impact, small reach, or small sales. In fact, Click Millionaires specialize in profiting from big-company–style systems but without out all the expense and hassle!

As popularized in Tim Ferris's now classic book, *The 4-Hour Workweek* (Crown Archetype, 2007), today you can use the Internet to construct job opportunities, projects, and even new companies around your own preferences. Even without a business background or a technical education you can design your career and business around your own schedule and interests instead of having to punch the clock at the same time and location every day, dressed the same way, interacting with the same people, and doing the same thing. Free worldwide email, phone, video, chat, and social networks now mean that you don't need to be physically present in an office much anymore.

The Internet allows free-flowing self-organizing projects and ventures to emerge constantly, reducing your dependence on corporate paychecks. Outsourcing, virtual assistants, freelance contractor project marketplaces, mobile platforms, social networks, telecommuting, browser-based SAAS tools, cloud computing . . . all of these developments have created a constant flow of new ventures and small business opportunities that don't require you to become a lifetime employee counting the years toward the gold watch you'll get when you retire.

What's a "Click Millionaire"?

I'm not talking about a "get-rich-quick" strategy. *Click Millionaires* is the manifesto of a movement focused on building flexible and profitable lifestyle businesses online that suit the individual lifestyle priorities of their Click Millionaire owners. Here's how I define the term:

> **Click Millionaire** [klik mil-*yuh*-**nair** *or* klik mil'ye-**nâr**] Click Millionaires use websites, e-commerce, digital publishing, and social media to build *lifestyle businesses* that share their ideas and products with the world on their own schedule and terms. *A lifestyle design movement* as much as a business model,

becoming a Click Millionaire does not require a million-dollar online business. Instead, Click Millionaires define success by using the latest digital commerce and marketing tools to build profitable, ethical, Internet-based businesses that improve their own lifestyles and the lives around them. The resulting *Click Millionaire lifestyles* offer unprecedented levels of personal career control, creative independence, schedule flexibility, and work satisfaction.

The traditional American dream centered on individual financial achievement—where becoming a "millionaire" allowed you to control your own life, afford anything you want, and live on your own terms. But today the phrase "Click Millionaire" captures the revolutionary idea that lifestyle benefits like the independence, security, and self-confidence—formerly only available to the wealthy—are now available to *anyone who chooses to build a successful lifestyle business online*. As you can see from the definition above, money is important to Click Millionaires, but it's not the only thing that matters to the "new rich." Money is not the destination on your life's road trip; it's just the gas to help you enjoy the journey.

To become a Click Millionaire I encourage you to:

- Change your thinking to focus first on your goal of living better, however you define that personally.

- Redesign your life around what's important to you and your family instead of working late to meet your boss's schedule.

- Rearrange your work so that your bank account benefits directly from your efforts instead of paying for your employers' new cars and vacations when you may be struggling to pay your mortgage.

My bet is that if you could redesign your life to emphasize your personal happiness, a comfortable lifestyle, and the ability to share your profits with others, you'd be satisfied—even without becoming a millionaire. Why? Because you're not greedy and the reality is that you would just like to be comfortable and lead a life that has meaning for you.

Don't Quit Working—Start Enjoying Your Work Instead

I'm not talking here about early retirement or passive income strategies. Instead what I'm proposing is that you start a business part-time, while you're still working your current job, and gradually build a *niche business online that generates recurring revenues for you as automatically as possible.* Over time you can grow your Click Millionaire side business to make an ever-increasing portion of your income, and a portion that you enjoy earning, too.

Wouldn't your life be easier with an extra $500 a month? How about $1,500 or $5,000 a month? Most business advice skips right over those more realistic numbers to promise you millions of dollars in some kind of magical cash transformation process. But Click Millionaires are realistic adults. We're not looking for *get-rich-quick* solutions. We look for legitimate opportunities that we can profit from with a reasonable amount of continuing hard work, clever marketing, and creativity. We invest our time to create profitable businesses that allow us the money and personal freedom to pursue lifestyles that we enjoy on a day-to-day basis, instead of only on weekends and during a few rushed weeks of vacation each year.

Everyone expects to be paid for their time. Where Click Millionaires differ is that they aim to evolve past the painful "hours for dollars" trade that dominates most people's working lives. Instead of organizing your life around working for someone else, as a Click

Millionaire you start with the premise that *you deserve to control your own time and daily schedule*. Your time is more valuable to you than to anyone else. If you are going to spend time on a project, then you deserve not only to be paid, but paid well.

But as a Click Millionaire, your success is not just financial. You want to invest your time in work you enjoy and that benefits your lifestyle. In most cases this means making more money, but in many cases this means doing less work so you can enjoy life, too. This is the real goal of Click Millionaires: *to get paid more for work you enjoy even while working less!*

I know this sounds ambitious or even crazy, but I have accomplished this personally. And, this book will share with you dozens more examples of Click Millionaire success that you can apply to your own life to become a member of the new rich, too.

Together we'll develop a plan to help you rearrange your life's priorities from making the boss rich to living a richer life yourself—not overnight but over time, part time. We'll explore digital business–building tools such as email newsletters, blogs, online communities, podcasting, online video, and affiliate marketing. All of these are fun and inexpensive business models you can take advantage of online starting today. And don't worry if all that sounds too technical. *Click Millionaires* introduces these opportunities in plain, nontechnical language that can help you learn to succeed on your own terms just like I have.

How can you redesign your life and start a lifestyle business to get your share of the Click Millionaires revolution? Read on!

2

passion vs. profits

setting your own lifestyle goals

When I went to school, they asked me what I wanted to be when I grew up. I wrote down "happy." They told me I didn't understand the assignment, and I told them they didn't understand life.

—John Lennon, musician

LIFESTYLE DESIGN means that today you can live in whatever world you choose to build for yourself. Today you can use the Internet to design your lifestyle and career around the interests, hobbies, and businesses that most interest you. And you can pursue this lifestyle design with less concern for location, capital, connections, or a boss's opinion than ever before.

To me, attending your child's school play, being able to go to the gym on a Thursday afternoon, visiting friends when it suits you, or finding time to take care of a sick relative is more important than attending the monthly staff meeting, making another sales call, or pushing for that last 10 percent of this quarter's production run. I'm not suggesting that you will stop working. Instead I'm suggesting that you create a new business that you enjoy working in, one that grows over time to more than pay your bills, and allows you greater independence, creative contribution, and flexibility in your daily schedule.

Unfortunately you have been programmed to ask for permission. From your earliest days in school, authority figures have been limiting your options for their own benefit. Your teachers made you sit still and respond to the lessons, your parents probably gave you a curfew, the government imposes taxes on your income, your neighbors expect you to behave like they do, and especially your boss requires specific performance, timely attendance, and participation in your work duties.

Imagine what could happen if you could stop asking for permission and instead began living your life on your own terms. What if you took the initiative to lead yourself toward a more lucrative and flexible future based on your own creativity?

What Kind of Lifestyle Benefits Am I Talking About?

By starting a business around your own interests, you officially give yourself permission to pursue the hobbies, projects, relationships, ideas, and products that interest you most.

As a Click Millionaire you don't have to ask someone else for permission to:

- Work from home.

- Dress for comfort, not to impress.

- Skip that dreadful commute.

‣ Vacation with your family whenever is convenient (and without negotiating with your co-workers and boss).

‣ Keep flexible schedules that allow more time for relationships or caregiving responsibilities.

‣ Take walks or run errands during the workday.

‣ Work outdoors or wherever your laptop takes you.

‣ Be available when the kids are sick or for school plays or parent–teacher conferences.

‣ Move to a warmer (or colder) climate.

‣ Reconnect with hobbies like playing an instrument, painting, or sports.

‣ Decorate your workspace to suit your personality.

‣ Visit the gym daily and the beach when the weather's nice.

‣ Be in charge of your own life, pursuing work that has personal meaning.

Imagine how much more productive and happier *your* life would be with lifestyle changes like these!

Taking charge of your own success is what becoming a Click Millionaire is all about.

Your Passion vs. Profits Balance

Enough money is certainly better than not enough, but I'll bet that financial security is not the only lifestyle change you're seeking. Independence, satisfying work, a flexible schedule, the opportunity to work with others, or even to be the boss—all those are important

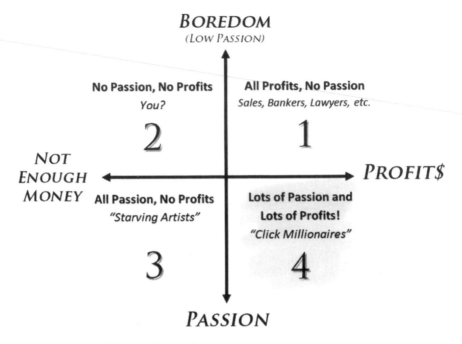

BOREDOM
(LOW PASSION)

No Passion, No Profits
You?

2

All Profits, No Passion
Sales, Bankers, Lawyers, etc.

1

NOT
ENOUGH
MONEY

PROFIT$

All Passion, No Profits
"Starving Artists"

3

Lots of Passion and
Lots of Profits!
"Click Millionaires"

4

PASSION

Figure 2–1. Click Millionaires Career Quadrants

parts of how you can choose to define success for yourself, a definition that goes far beyond just increasing your paychecks.

What you really need in your life is *balance*. Many people get caught up overdoing it when pursuing either money or their personal passion.

Many regular folks (maybe you?) find themselves stuck in Quadrant 2 of the Click Millionaires Career Quadrants chart shown in Figure 2–1. This is the land of wage slaves. They are required to work lots of hours on tasks that don't empower them but they still can't ever quite make enough money to really get ahead.

You can also see that too much passion without enough profits can land you in Click Millionaires Career Quadrant 3 as a "Starving Artist." Starving artists and people who spend too much time "doing their own thing" often find themselves broke if they ignore their finances.

The opposite is Quadrant 1, where those who are solely profit-driven work. They make enough money, maybe even more than enough, but often lead one-dimensional lives or they are unhappily dependent on the firm for their lifestyles. Too much emphasis on money alone often leaves unhappy investment bankers, salespeople, and workaholics feeling trapped in this money-first Quadrant.

I want to help you balance your life between passion and profits better. As a Click Millionaire you can build a profitable business that also allows you both the income and flexibility to lead the life you deserve.

This means helping you graduate to Quadrant 4. In Quadrant 4 you are a Click Millionaire; you enjoy the time you invest in your work and your passion for it is rewarded financially, too.

The Click Millionaires Investment Mindset

One of the first steps on the road to Click Millionaire success is to recognize the value of your own time. You have the opportunity to *invest* your time instead of just *spending* it. Even if you only have a few hours to yourself each week after your work obligations are finished, the Internet can help you. Of course you can waste that time online just surfing around, playing *Angry Birds*, or watching goofy videos on YouTube. Or you can invest that time in learning new skills, making new friends and business contacts, and turning your hobbies into businesses.

The Internet is available 24/7, so you can move your life forward and redesign it bit by bit by bit even if it's only in 10- or 15-minute increments late at night, after work, or on weekends after you put the kids to bed.

This "investment" mindset is key to your long-term success as a Click Millionaire. Even if you don't have tons of free time or money, you still have the opportunity and ability to set long-term goals and redesign your life, changing it gradually over time to build yourself an online business that helps you upgrade your lifestyle.

In the real world, success is rightfully more often measured in happiness like this than in stock options. Happiness, free time, a schedule that allows for family and friends, meaningful work without a lot of hassle, and ideally enough money left over to enjoy some luxuries and help those less fortunate, too.

Doesn't that sound like a better way to live?

Comparison of Three Lifestyle Paths

Figure 2–2 shows a quick comparison of the lifestyle impact and happiness of three paths: working for someone else; starting your own company; or following a Click Millionaires strategy.

THREE LIFESTYLE PATHS

Working for a Company	Traditional Start-up Approach	Click Millionaires Strategy
• Collect paychecks with little upside potential	• Have a brilliant idea and take responsibility for starting a new company	• Build profitable projects that support your lifestyle and allow you to pursue your interests
• Follow management's growth decisions	• Raise money from outside investors	• Fund yourself (bootstrap)
• Commute to the office daily	• Share ownership and authority	• Keep control for yourself
• Meetings	• Hire people to grow the company as quickly as possible	• Focus on profitability and lifestyle instead of growth
• Work to meet goals set by your boss	• Manage employees	• Work from home or wherever you like
• More meetings	• Pay overhead costs for office, parking, furniture, insurance, etc.	• No commute
• Support boss's dreams of getting rich	• Commute daily	• Little to no office overhead costs
• Live for the weekend	• Lots of meetings	• Few or no meetings
• Hope to survive downsizings	• Work very hard for years hoping to make yourself and investors rich by selling out via merger or IPO	• Freelance contractors (less expensive than staff)
• Hope to save enough for retirement	• Try to retire young	• Work on projects you like
• Wonder if life is passing you by . . .	• Wonder what to do next if you succeed	• Work with people you like
	• Start all over if you don't . . .	• Build assets and recurring income for yourself
		• Position for long-term happiness rather than sale
		• Enjoy sharing your success with others
		• Love your work enough to never want to retire!
OKAY	**BETTER**	**BEST**

Figure 2–2.

. . . . . . 3 . . . . . .

how to redesign your life and business

If you don't design your own life plan, chances are you'll fall into someone else's plan. And guess what they have planned for you? Not much.
—Jim Rohn, U.S. entrepreneur,
author, and motivational speaker

THE SIZE AND SHAPE and flavor of your Click Millionaire lifestyle depends on the kind of business you choose to build. The profits, growth potential, and fun level of that business are up to you and the kind of Click Millionaire systems you design into it.

Start with your own lifestyle goals and put your personal priorities first. The fundamental questions that only *you* can answer are:

‣ How do you want to spend your days?

‣ What do you most like to do?

‣ What kind of contribution do you want to make to the world?

Once you've answered those questions, you need to do the equally hard work of figuring out what you need to *change* in your current life to make room for these new things. While positive changes are the most fun to consider, there may be negative things in your life or work that need to be addressed first. If so, it's likely that you need to clear some space before you can make any other changes. Or, you may need to stop doing some things you think are valuable to allow room in your life to try new things.

So, how to get there from here?

Choosing Your Own World

Today you have more flexibility to arrange your life in just the way you want than at any time in history. In the 20th century you had to "toe the line" when working for a big company. Because companies prioritize their needs and profits ahead of yours, they require you to follow their schedules, their rules, their schemes for advancement, their supervision; you need to accept their pay, and get their permission for any deviation.

Today all that's not as necessary. I know that you have been taught that prioritizing your own lifestyle conveniences is "not professional." But when you run your own business, *you* get to decide what's professional.

Today you can begin choosing your own world starting in your free time, part-time. Even if you're working for someone else, you have some free time, too. What do you do after hours? If you're not careful you'll fritter your time away. Everybody has the same 24 hours in a day and 7 days in a week, but different people accomplish different things with that time.

Look at reallocating that time to invest it in projects that will pay you back a financial or personal satisfaction return. Choose your hobbies, your entertainment, the books you read, and even your friends a little more carefully than you did before.

Even if you have job or family obligations that restrict you to certain hours or a specific location, the Internet offers you access to the whole world. There are billions of people out there whom you can reach with a few clicks of the mouse or pecks at the keyboard at any time day or night. The Internet has lowered the costs of communication and collaboration so the risks of entrepreneurship are lower now, too.

How to Start Investing Your Free Time

So how are you going to choose to *invest* your free time to build the lifestyle you want? Get online. At first maybe you can only squeeze out an extra 10 minutes a day. But go online and spend your time with purpose, researching the niches, websites, and communities online that you want to build your lifestyle around. If you invest that daily 10 minutes in studying marine biology, meeting Italian chefs, or learning PHP programming, over time you will make progress toward your lifestyle goals and begin laying the foundation for an online lifestyle business. As Click Millionaire Connie Mettler, entrepreneur and publisher of ArtFairCalendar.com has said, "Keep piling up your grains of sand, soon you'll have a castle."

Let's talk about specifics: Say your dream is to learn to speak French and travel regularly to Paris, maybe even live there. But you're trapped in a soul-killing day job—stuck in a 7-Eleven in Albuquerque or working as a cubicle slave for a big corporation in Minneapolis. You're not happy where you are; you dream of upgrading your life to include speaking French and eventually even living and working in France. How are you going to build that new lifestyle?

I understand that you don't have the money to just walk away, but you can reorient your free time to invest it toward this kind of lifestyle goal. When you come home from work, what if you started reorienting your free time toward people, activities, culture, and business opportunities that were... French? Instead of spending your time after hours just watching TV or playing World of Warcraft or Farmville, how about instead investing it online to meet French people, learn the language, and generally pursuing French-ness? All the information and people you need are available online right now. A simple search on Google can get you started. This is not abstract theory—it's not "envision it and abundance will magically appear." This is "come home from work, get on the computer, and find a bunch of French websites to get started."

Build Yourself a Different Life Online

There are lots of French people in the United States and around the world who speak English. And there are lots of English speakers living in France. And they are online. They're on Facebook right now, they're writing and reading and commenting on blogs, they're participating in communities online where you and your French interests would be welcome. There are French videos on YouTube and podcasts you can download, too.

Whether French is your thing or not, it's just an example. Instead you may want to become a black belt in karate, start a new landscaping business, restore old cars, found a recycling business, or become a YouTube video star.

The point is, you can do any of these things or whatever else you put your mind to, if you start investing time in it. So how about going to Google and finding out about something you want to learn more about? And starting to participate in the blogs, websites, communities, and podcasts for your interest? I'll bet you can find some people online who would be happy to get to know you because you're interested in the same things.

To continue our example, suppose that after a few weeks of online browsing and participation, you make some friends who speak French. You start spending your free time learning French with them; maybe reading French books (easy kids books at first!); you start watching some French TV online; and practicing your French in online forums, too. Maybe some of your new friends even live in Paris.

You start paying attention to what your new friends like, the kinds of products and services they recommend or are looking for. You start a blog, a video series, a promotional service, or even just begin doing part-time work as a virtual assistant for your new French friends (all of these Click Millionaire business models are discussed later in the book).

Keep at it nightly online to extend your network (social networks make this easier than ever before). Find the French people you want to play and work with. Soon you have friends who live in France. Some of those people you meet online might be visiting your neighborhood, they might come over to see you and get better acquainted. Your French gets even better. What kind of people live and work, or at least vacation, in Paris? People who have friends in France, and now you do! Next they might even invite you over to visit them *in France*.

Your French keeps improving, you make more friends, and you learn your way around the culture and community. Drawing on the Click Millionaire business skills this book teaches and your unique cross-cultural perspective, you start to see niche business opportunities that are invisible to outsiders. On a part-time basis and with the support of your new French friends, you use the Internet to start providing them information, services, or products that serve their needs—and make you some money, too.

You're on your way to becoming a business owner and a respected French expert online. Each night after you clock out from day job, you're stepping into an increasingly French lifestyle without having quit your job or leaving your home in Albuquerque.

Welcome to the World of Lifestyle Design

Voila! You created a lifestyle where you're hanging out with French people and making money, just as you dreamed about. You have redefined success for yourself outside your day job. You invested your time online by learning to speak some French and redesigned your life forever.

If you invest your time wisely like this, it turns out you can create the opportunities, build the lifestyle, and choose the world you want to live in. This is *lifestyle design*—you use the Internet to open doors, expand your horizons, and fulfill your own needs.

You can do this—you can reorient the world around where you want to be and how you want to live. *You can choose the world you live in.* What do you want? It's all out there with a few mouse clicks and some cleverly invested time. It's not magic, it's applied motivation. You take small but consistent steps and you get there, bit by bit. And the more you get involved in the culture, the community, or the business arenas in which you want to participate, the more you build relationships with other people. And the more relationships you have, the more business opportunities arrive.

How long does this take? And what kind of return can you expect from this strategy? That depends on how you invest your time. But I suggest *investing* your free time like this in activities that feed the larger goals of your life rather than just *spending* it like most people do. I'm certain that a lot more is going to happen with this approach than if you just sit on your couch, watch TV, feel sorry for yourself, or complain to your friends.

Invest your life better, smarter. Change your world. Redesign it to become the Click Millionaire you want to be.

click millionaires lifestyle design exercises

The master in the art of living makes little distinction between his work and his play, his labor and his leisure, his mind and his body, his information and his recreation, his love and his religion. He hardly knows which is which. He simply pursues his vision of excellence at whatever he does, leaving others to decide whether he is working or playing. To him he's always doing both.
—James A. Michener, U.S. novelist

WHAT WOULD YOUR ideal Click Millionaire lifestyle look like if you "made it" running your own business?

Imagine your life, your day-to-day routine, your house, your living arrangements, your car, etc.

What changes would you want to make to your current life to get there? What are you happy with today and what would you like to upgrade?

From these mental pictures you can decide your priorities. What are the easy things to change, the ones that are somewhat harder, and the difficult obstacles that will require the most work?

As your own boss you can do what you like best and outsource the rest, allowing you to enjoy both your work and your life more.

The following lifestyle design exercises are the first of several sets of exercises in this book. Their goal is to help you identify the activities and people you like (and don't like!). By clarifying your lifestyle preferences and goals up-front, you can prioritize them when redesigning your life and business so that you not only make more money but increase your flexibility, independence, creativity, fulfillment, and fun, too.

Keep in mind, these exercises can only help you if you actually do them! Just thinking through them is not nearly as good as writing down your answers.

Your Click Millionaires Idea Journal

Now that you are on your way to becoming a Click Millionaire, you are training yourself to think more analytically and spot new business opportunities in the world around you. Unfortunately, insight doesn't always strike when it's convenient—great new ideas may hit you when you're on the freeway, at the grocery, in the bathroom, or even in the middle of the night. The best time to capture these inspirations is as soon as they appear, so it's important that you develop the habit of writing down anything and everything that occurs to you. Don't be embarrassed to start listening to your own inner voices. Not all of the ideas will be good but you need to write them down as soon as you have them. Even the most seemingly obvious ideas will fade from your memory as soon as you are distracted.

So one of my top Click Millionaires success tools is a *simple notebook*.

I keep a pad of paper by my bed. I am often surprised and pleased in the morning to wake up and find barely legible scribbles that detail new business ideas. I suggest you do the same. You can use any old notebook or buy an official one online at www.ClickMillionaires IdeaJournal.com. Keep your Idea Journal with you at all times. You might want a big one for your desk and a small one for your purse, your car, or bedside table. (My wife even bought me an underwater scuba diving writing slate a few years ago. It's surprising how often valuable ideas occur when I'm in the shower!) You can also record your latest brainstorms on your mobile phone using voice recording apps or by calling your own voicemail. Just be sure that you then transcribe your voicemails later by writing them down into your notebook. You want to collect all of your ideas in one place where you can review them easily and be inspired to develop them further.

Every time I mention your Click Millionaires Idea Journal, please put your notebook to use by writing down your ideas and responses to the book's exercises. As you progress through the chapters and make an honest attempt to participate in all the exercises, you'll soon see those pages filling up with insights that could change your life.

....

LIFESTYLE DESIGN EXERCISES: PART ONE

To get your lifestyle redesign thought process started, brainstorm answers to the following questions. Be sure to write your answers down in your Click Millionaires Idea Journal so you can develop your strategy over time.

Income:
- How much money do I want?
- How much money do I actually need each year?
- How would my financial situation change if I worked from home?

If I didn't need to work at all, I would invest my time in:

▸ These 5 favorite activities

▸ These 5 favorite places

If 1,000 fans were paying me $100 each annually, what would I do for them?

Complete the paragraph below:

My ideal day would begin at __ o'clock in the city of _____. I would wake up and start my day by doing _____. Then I would _____. By dinnertime I would have accomplished _____, _____, and _____. I would do that by working with _____, _____, and _____. I would also leave time for _____, _____, and _____ before I went to bed, including time to help _____ do _____.

Current Lifestyle Questions

▸ Why do you live where you live? Would you like to change that?

▸ What limits have you placed on your own life and behavior that may not be fair to you?

▸ Which of your daily activities are old-fashioned habits and routines that are unnecessary today?

▸ Which of your recurring self-criticisms or self-doubts are not fair to you and the potential you represent?

▸ Which of your behaviors are in reaction to events of your childhood or incidents in your past that you could and should have let go of long ago?

▸ How could you redesign your lifestyle to address these issues and improve your day-to-day happiness?

Feel free to write down multiple answers for any question in your Click Millionaires Idea Journal or revisit these questions repeatedly. The more you document about your personal lifestyle goals, the more we will have to work with as your lifestyle redesign process continues.

Your Lifestyle Activity Goals

Even if your Click Millionaire business grows to keep you busy full-time, you still have the option to prioritize your workday activities around the lifestyle you choose to design. After all, you're the boss! Here are some examples to help you crystallize your general desires into concrete activities. You can design any of these lifestyle choices into the daily operations of your new business to start upgrading your day-to-day life:

▸ I want to sleep later.

▸ I want to take summers off.

▸ I want to travel more (or less).

▸ I want to be able to take my kids to school each morning.

▸ I want to have time to finish my degree in . . .

▸ I want to own a horse.

▸ I want to lose 50 pounds.

▸ I want to play hockey at least 1 hour every day.

▸ I want to learn to speak Italian.

- I want to volunteer at my church soup kitchen at least once each month.

- I want to dress casually at work.

- I want to work from home.

- I want to be able to choose who I work with.

- I want to stop doing _____ kinds of projects.

- I want to cut my commute in half.

- I want to meet new people through my work.

- I want my work to involve travel (or fine dining, scuba diving, antique bottle collecting, helping the elderly, or . . .).

- I want to be able to take Thursdays off to work in my garden.

LIFESTYLE DESIGN EXERCISES: PART TWO

My favorite things are:

- 5 favorite hobbies
- 5 favorite work or work-related activities
- 5 favorite places
- 5 favorite types of projects
- 5 favorite types of people

In my life I want more of:

- 5 leisure activities
- 5 work-related activities
- 5 material objects

In my life I want less of:

- 5 current job activities

▸ 5 current personal activities

▸ 5 certain people or types of people

Short-term goals:

In the next six months the 5 things I would most like to change are . . .

Long-term goals:

In the next 24 months the 5 things I would most like to change are . . .

....

Lifestyle Perks of Click Millionaires

When it's your business you can make money doing things that you like so much that you might normally pay to do them. It becomes part of your "job" to pursue opportunities and build relationships in the fields that interest you. This can lead to exciting, prestigious, and surprising lifestyle bonuses along the way.

For example:

▸ Sid Kreis (of online pool and billiards retailer Seyberts.com) gets to hang out with his heroes—the top pool players in the world.

▸ Connie Mettler (of ArtFairInsiders.com and ArtFairCalendar .com) gets to be a judge at the art fairs she loves, and people stop her on the street at art fairs to give her donations to keep her websites going.

▸ Al Peterson, publisher of broadcasting industry email newsletter *NTS Media Online*, gets to host his own annual conference with celebrity guest speakers.

▸ Online community owner Rob Ludlow (of Backyard Chickens.com) and podcaster Betty Thesky (of Bettyinthe

SkywithaSuitcase.com) both got book deals to share their expertise with readers worldwide.

› I get interviewed on radio and TV, and organizations fly me around the world to consult on entrepreneurship, strategy, and to speak at their events.

All of these fun activities count as "doing business" when you design your own business to include them.

What are the perks of your favorite industry or hobby that you would like to enjoy?

› Speaking gigs.

› Free review copies of new products.

› Free attendance at conferences.

› Invitations to VIP events.

› Being quoted in the press as an "expert."

› Selling your own branded products.

› Fan mail.

› Book deals.

› Fundraising for your favorite charity.

Don't forget to share your thoughts with your Click Millionaires Idea Journal.

LIFESTYLE DESIGN EXERCISES: PART THREE

Now that you are focused on the lifestyle issues most important to you, here are several final lifestyle design exercises to help develop a personalized action plan.

1. Brainstorm: Drawing on the exercises you've already completed, start a detailed new brainstorming list of 20 likes and 20 dislikes about your life and work situations. It may be a challenge but force yourself to brainstorm 20 of *each* to write down in your Click Millionaires Idea Journal.

2. Prioritize: Prioritize each list in rank order to show the top likes you most want to add to or preserve from your current life and the top dislikes that you would most like to change.

3. Evaluate: Of your top likes, which of your desired changes are the most easily accomplished? (You can't make yourself taller, for example, but you could move out of town to live on a lake. So eliminate "be taller" or other impossibilities from your likes list.)

Now look closely at the top 10 dislikes on your list, too. Of the top dislikes, which are the ones most easily avoided?

4. Combine and rerank: Take the top 10 most important and easily accomplished likes and add them to your top 10 most important and changeable dislikes to create a new combined list of 20 entries.

Rank in order the new combined list to reflect the importance and priority of both likes and dislikes. Chop off the 10 lowest-ranked ones to create a top 10 list of both likes and dislikes that shows your most desired lifestyle changes that are both possible and doable.

5. Take a break: Sleep on this list. Revisit your top 10 lifestyle changes list tomorrow or again next weekend.

6. Reevaluate: When you're ready, revisit your list of the 10 most important lifestyle changes. How does it look to you now? What did you miss? Do any new ones come to mind that deserve to be on the list? Rearrange the list to put the easiest lifestyle design changes or the most important ones nearer to the top. Do those priorities reflect a life you would like to lead?

If you've done these exercises correctly, you should be close to creating the personalized game plan for redesigning your life that I call your Lifestyle Design Shopping List.

CLICK MILLIONAIRES SECRET: You Don't Need to Go It Alone

Making changes in your life takes courage and commitment over time. That's why it's easier to do with friends along for the ride. As you go through this process, try to find a friend or relative who can support you. Feedback from someone else's perspective can be very helpful in clarifying and accomplishing your goals.

Many people are afraid to discuss their new business ideas with work colleagues because their boss might hear about it. And many others have friends willing to listen but those friends don't enough business background or Internet experience to help.

If this sounds like your situation, come to ClickMillionaires.com. I started this friendly social network specifically to mentor aspiring entrepreneurs like you and help you help one another, too. I'm there in the Forum daily myself coaching people and answering the questions you're probably asking.

Your membership is free with purchase of this book, so let us help you at www.ClickMillionairesReader.com!

Sign Here

Your Lifestyle Design Shopping List

Now that you've thought through the likes and dislikes of your current life, and explored the lifestyle changes that are most meaningful to you, it's time to summarize. Return to your Click Millionaires Idea Journal to create a final list that will generate your answers to the following questions:

▸ What are the most important priorities for you in a redesigned daily routine?

▸ What activities, projects, or people are the most important for you to feel you are "succeeding" in your life?

Rank in order these top lifestyle goals. This is your new Lifestyle Design Shopping List. The more of these activities and priorities that you can include in your redesigned Click Millionaire lifestyle, the happier you will be!

In Part Two, let's look at the business opportunities you can find online today to support your new lifestyle goals. We'll come back to your Lifestyle Design Shopping List to integrate those goals into your new business model in a later chapter, too.

PART TWO
CLICK MILLIONAIRES
LIFESTYLE BUSINESS SYSTEMS

. . . . . . 5 . . . . . .

click millionaires lifestyle business design success principles

BUILDING A PROFITABLE new business is never easy, but Click Millionaires implement e-commerce and advertising-based online business models that use outsourcing, software, and automated online marketing to build systems that generate recurring revenues with as little daily work required as possible.

The goal of a Click Millionaire "business system" is for you to create a "virtuous cycle" of easily expanded, self-reinforcing, and profitable business processes. The more customers you have, the more money you make. That supports more product development and marketing. The better products and marketing you have, the more customers you attract. Then the more customers you attract, etc. As the system grows ("scales"), Click Millionaires make more money but with proportionately *less* work.

That's a Click Millionaire business system!

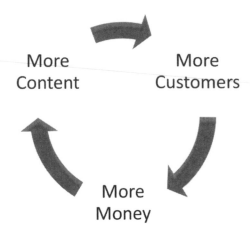

Figure 5–1. *Virtuous Cycle*

How to Make Money Online: Basic Business Models

You're probably familiar with these e-commerce concepts, but for those who are new to e-business, there are three basic ways to make money online:

Sell physical goods: This is like traditional retail sales but the orders are taken online instead of face-to-face in a store, by mail, or over the phone.

Sell digital goods: E-books, documents, software, recordings, or subscription content can be delivered as digital files downloaded from the Internet. Access to membership websites falls in this category, too.

Sell advertising: Ads can be placed in blogs, forums, email newsletters, or other digital media.

(We'll get into more details on how to make and collect money for each type later in the book.)

Click Millionaires implement these business models to build their own automated business systems online with little staff or investment. This is the real goal of Click Millionaires—*to create a sustainable business system personalized to your interests, skills, and lifestyle goals.*

Combining these business approaches with the Click Millionaires Lifestyle Business Design Success Principles detailed below can help you develop a profitable product you believe in, a cost-effective production method you enjoy, and a customer-attraction strategy that includes fun activities with people you like, all wrapped into an honest, interesting Internet-based business that can also "scale" to create more money for you with little additional effort required.

How Click Millionaires Create New Markets

Here's an overview of how to develop the personalized business system you need to become a Click Millionaire:

1. Find a niche that does not have much competition and that is underserved.

"Underserved" means that the target market is not having its niche needs fully met. You can build a business around helping the people in that niche by delivering better information or products, ideally products or services that serve big recurring needs like helping them make more money, improving their lives, or solving their problems.

Where these niche strategies differ from traditional approaches is that they speak specifically to the niche needs or point of view of your target customers better than preexisting mass market alternatives.

2. Communicate as much as you have time for online to spread your brand and marketing messages. But don't start selling right away; your goal is develop a loyal audience first and monetize later.

3. Create content or entertainment or services that attract that audience back on a regular basis and that inspires them to tell their friends.

4. Offer solutions to their problems. These might be direct solutions, like a better flea powder for dog owners or an office workout bike like the Fitdesk that helps you lose weight while working. They might be information products you create, like an e-book of tips on how to fix Harley Davidson motorcycles or an illustrated "word of the day" to help kids learn to read. They might be personal services you offer, like graphic design or life coaching by phone. Or they might simply be ads from other companies that sell products/services your audience appreciates.

That's really all there is to it but this is no overnight solution. Serving peoples' needs requires you to invest time, energy, and especially creativity to address their problems in ways that are better than those that were available before you started your business. But if you do those things, and deliver quality products tailored to your niche, over time you can build a profitable audience where others *didn't even realize one existed!*

The Lifestyle Business Design
Success Principles of Click Millionaires

To build these profitable audiences, Click Millionaires design their business systems with special attention to the factors discussed below. Designing your business around these key principles can upgrade an average business into a profitable Click Millionaire lifestyle business system for you.

CLICK MILLIONAIRES SUCCESS PRINCIPLE #1: HELP PEOPLE

The best place to start a business is where people need help. Finding demand for products and services is a smarter investment of your time than researching suppliers of products that nobody may want. This may sound obvious but I've seen far too many entrepreneurs miss it. They focus so narrowly on promoting ideas or products related to their own passions that they skip right over this fundamental requirement. If you serve a need outside of your own need to make money by helping people solve problems, make more money, lose weight, feel better, or enjoy their lives more, you are far more likely to find recurring, profitable customers.

Dedication to helping people can help you market your business, too. As your happy customers tell their friends, your business grows more cheaply than if you have to pay for advertising to acquire new customers. Creating a relationship of long-term value where the customer depends on your business for something important is also one of the best ways to survive changes in the marketplace.

CLICK MILLIONAIRES SUCCESS PRINCIPLE #2: EXPERT CREDIBILITY

People prefer to buy things from those that they perceive as "experts." Doctors, lawyers, accountants, and professors are familiar examples of experts, as are plumbers, personal trainers, master gardeners, astrologers, auto mechanics, etc.

Today a new type of expert—the "trusted friend"—is emerging. You can use your own real-life experiences and expertise to position yourself as one of this new breed of experts online, even if you don't have "official" expert credibility. Establishing yourself, your business, and your website as a credible authority in whatever field you are serving will help you make money online.

This topic is so important that Chapter 6 is entirely about how you can achieve expert status quickly online.

CLICK MILLIONAIRES SUCCESS PRINCIPLE #3: AUTOMATION

Automation means that you don't have to perform repetitive functions yourself. Instead, those tasks are performed automatically, usually by software or by human assistance when necessary. As the industrial revolution introduced automated production to build great fortunes for the men at the top of their organizations, today you can use software to automate many business functions and create recurring profits for yourself with few to no employees.

Examples of automation include:

‣ *Ordering and delivery:* E-commerce purchasing has become so common that we forget what a huge time- and money-saver it is to let websites take and deliver orders instead of human clerks.

‣ *Content creation and production:* Blogs, forum software, and social networks all allow your audience to leave comments and interact with each other without your participation required.

‣ *Customer service:* Customers solve their own problems by consulting FAQ ("Frequently Asked Questions") web pages or online user support communities.

‣ *Billing:* Customers pay online so money arrives in your bank account automatically.

‣ *Marketing:*

  – Online ads are automatically displayed to search engine users looking for information on products like yours.

  – Autoresponder email messages automatically follow up (repeatedly) with prospects to generate more sales.

  – Data feeds spread your messages across platforms (e.g., from your blog to Twitter to Facebook, etc.) automatically.

Web-based tools like these can be used to run your business, attract sales and generate revenues even when you are not "on duty." *A properly constructed Click Millionaire business system uses automation to create a worldwide sales force that never sleeps!*

CLICK MILLIONAIRES SUCCESS PRINCIPLE #4: OUTSOURCING

Today you don't need all the physical infrastructure of traditional business—no storefront, office, furniture, parking, insurance, etc. You also can keep costs down by not hiring full-time employees. In fact it can be a lot more efficient and cheaper to only hire contractors for each kind of specific project you need completed. Part-time and freelance-based help can be found for any project today at sites like Elance.com, Guru.com, oDesk.com, and Freelancer.com. These online project marketplaces are like eBay but instead of selling old stuff from your garage, you post your business projects. Individual contractors from all over the world will offer you bids to help. With just a few clicks, you can hire copywriters, website designers, customer service reps, lawyers, salespeople, graphic artists, social media marketers, and more. (In Chapter 17 we'll discuss how you can become a Click Millionaire yourself by filling demand for these types of project-based and part-time services.)

I recommend finding good virtual assistants online to handle any of the repetitive tasks your website business creates that can't be automated with software. Now that you're the boss, you can back yourself up with staff to do anything you don't know how to do (or don't want to do!), and it's probably tax deductible, too. You will be better off investing $10, $20, or even $50/hour to pay others to handle the "small stuff" while you conserve your valuable time to work on bigger projects and enjoy your life more.

**CLICK MILLIONAIRES SUCCESS PRINCIPLE #5:
AUDIENCE CONTENT CREATION**

Audience content creation is when participation from your audience helps to create your products for you.

Examples of valuable audience-generated content can include:

› Comments on your blog.

▸ Guest posts submitted by audience members.

▸ Forum or discussion board conversations.

▸ Photo or video sharing uploads.

▸ Classified ads or personal profile listings.

▸ Reviews of products.

▸ Directory information entries.

These audience contributions are valuable because they create more content that other potential customers visit your site to see. With more visitors you'll make more money from advertising and sell more of your own products, too.

CLICK MILLIONAIRES SUCCESS PRINCIPLE #6: SCALABILITY

Automation, outsourcing, and audience content creation are all examples of a key Click Millionaires concept called "scalability."

> **scalability** [skāl-uh-**bil**-i-tee]: The ability of a technology or business system to adapt easily to increased volume and to maintain or improve profitability without requiring significant additional resources.

In plain English, "scaling well" means that your business can grow without requiring lots more money and with less of your personal involvement, too. Many small businesses fail because their owners don't plan ahead for how their business will scale to handle more customers. If they are too personally involved in serving each new client they end up doing added work for each additional customer. Soon they can serve no more customers and their business stops growing (or even collapses because the founder got stretched too thin).

So while you want to work hard to get your first sale, and even your first 100 sales, you should design your business so that additional customers after that take little or no more effort from you. This is where the software and automated marketing techniques of the Internet can kick in to build the profitable lifestyle businesses that create true Click Millionaires; a scalable business system will keep making sales automatically online without requiring proportionately more work from you.

CLICK MILLIONAIRES SUCCESS PRINCIPLE #7: RECURRING REVENUES
One of the best ways to make more money, more easily online today is to replace one-time sales with automatically renewing subscriptions. This means that customers pay you not just once but repeatedly over time! Whether your venture is business-to-business or business-to-consumer, this approach can save you tons of time. Instead of requiring you to remarket to those customers, resell them, negotiate new deals, send more invoices, and then chase them for payment each time, customers give you their credit card numbers up front with permission to charge them again on a regular basis. A weekly subscription to your email newsletter, a monthly membership in your forum, a bimonthly shipment of a consumable product, a quarterly pass to some exclusive content, an annual software license or advertising renewal—those are all subscription commerce strategies.

For example, instead of selling an e-book for $100, you could repackage the first half of the book into a $75 up-front cost and then charge $35 for additional chapters every following month. Or you can offer ads on your site but instead of charging $500 once, you might charge $375 up-front and $150 every following month until the advertiser cancels.

Switching the "default" from you having to chase customers for more revenues to them having to cancel can make a huge difference in your daily activities and revenues. If your service continues to deliver value each month, this approach can yield more profit because you keep billing the customer's credit card every month, potentially forever. I've personally used this recurring revenue strategy with great success, especially for advertising and membership sales. By switching from manual invoices and renewals to automated subscription billing, Click Millionaires can turn the administrative headache of constantly asking clients and advertisers for money into a super easy—and usually more profitable—revenue stream instead. That also frees you to focus on the fun stuff—content and community and relationships and vacations—instead of sales and collecting accounts receivable.

Compounding Recurring Revenues—Where the Magic Happens!

If you grow your business to have a stable base of subscribers, this can mean thousands of dollars of income each month recurring automatically. Why? Simply because many people don't cancel! They invested time in researching your offer, going through the sign-up process, and hopefully enjoying your product or services. At that point inertia is on your side: Many people allow subscriptions to keep billing them rather than taking the time to cancel. This quirk of human behavior can make you a lot of money.

And, if you can acquire new subscription-based customers faster than you lose old ones, your income will not only recur every month but grow, too.

TRADITIONAL BILLING FOR A ONE-TIME $25 PRODUCT SALE

100 customers × $25 each = $2,500 one-time revenue.

If you have done all your marketing to attract those customers, why stop there? Just like your cable TV and cell phone companies long ago figured out, changing the credit card billing authorization from "one time" to "subscription" can continue to make money from those initial sales for as long as you keep providing enough value to keep customers from canceling.

RECURRING BILLING FOR A SUBSCRIPTION AT $20 UP FRONT + $5/MONTH

100 customers $\times$ $20 each = $2,000 one-time revenue.

Yes, that's less than you made in the one time sale example, but recurring revenues start in the following months. Even if some of those original customers cancel their subscriptions in each following month, you'll make $5.00 more from each of them every month until they do. So from that initial 100 customers you'd likely earn something like $500 more the second month, plus $400 the third month (assuming some customers cancel), plus $300 the fourth month (assuming some more customers cancel), and on and on. There are likely to be some customers who never cancel, allowing you to keep charging their cards for as long as you keep delivering the service or product they subscribed to. That can change a one-time $2,500 sale to thousands more dollars over time. And if you keep adding new subscribers each month, too, you can grow a base of long-term subscribers who continue to pay you monthly for years.

If you design this subscription billing strategy into your product and services it can make a huge difference both to your bank account and to your daily lifestyle as a business owner.

‣ ‣ ‣

Put all seven of these proven Click Millionaires Lifestyle Business Design Success Principles together and you get a business that is:

‣ low maintenance

‣ low cost

‣ sustainable

› scalable

› with recurring revenues

That success frees you to start more businesses with what you learn from this book or just enjoy your new Click Millionaire lifestyle.

> **Shhh . . . Wanna Know a Secret?**
> How about a Click Millionaires Secret that I have saved just for you as a reader of this book?
>
> To get my latest online marketing discovery for free, please visit www. Click MillionairesSecret.com.

strategies to position yourself as a niche expert online today

When self-promotion is done right, it's help. Help everyone.

—Tweet from Peter Shankman,
founder of HelpaReporterOut.com

EACH OF US HAS knowledge that is valuable to someone else somewhere. But historically it hasn't always been easy to find the people who need your info or share your interests. The Internet helps eliminate the traditional barriers to information distribution like geography, time zones, and cost, liberating you to share your knowledge with the world.

As noted in Chapter 5's Click Millionaires Success Principle #2, a helpful strategy for profiting from this age of unprecedented person-to-person interaction and its resulting commerce is by positioning yourself as an "expert." If your ideas, viewpoints, products, advice, or services are valuable enough for people to pay for, then even if those people are only a tiny percentage of the available audience online, you have a potentially *huge* Internet-based business.

Here's a guide to quickly establishing yourself as the "go-to" expert in your chosen target market, even without a fancy degree.

How to Compete as an Expert Today

The Internet has democratized access to information. The answers to most questions are now available online instantly for free. Search engines dive deep into university libraries to share details of the most technical subjects, and YouTube serves up videos of cutting-edge lectures and conference presentations on all sorts of topics for free. At the same time social networks and specialized blogs and forums help share information on even the most specialized topics. If everybody can learn everything online, how do you compete as an expert?

1. *Offer authentic, specialized expertise so that you can really help people.* This expertise doesn't need to be unique or based on formal academic credentials anymore. I'll explain why today's best opportunities are in niche markets and discuss the "new breed" of experts shortly.

2. *Offer solutions; don't just give advice.* It's easier to sell solutions than general advice because anyone with a problem is motivated to solve it. And that implies that they're ready to pay you the money or give you the attention your business needs. While general advice on saving time, saving money, looking better, or making more money is helpful, individualized answers and personalized solutions to niche problems are harder to find and therefore more valuable.

3. *Take advantage of social media and its more friendly style to personalize your expert advice and deliver it in an engaging way.* There's always demand for expert advice that helps people apply the textbook answers to the specific situations of their own lives. If you combine that with a more personal, helpful, and authentic approach than the formal, academic experts of generations past, you can help people, make money, and have fun online, too. Today's experts go to where the customers are—they hang out on Facebook, answer questions on Twitter or Quora, share personal news on Google+, and blog not only about their business or lifestyle topics but inject humor and personal updates, too.

Your Expertise Does Not Have to Be Unique

There is room for millions of niche experts providing personalized services online today, including you. By definition personalized services require personal attention to create and deliver. That means that even if there are 100 or more competitors already active online in your niche, it's not likely that they can reliably serve more than 100 customers each. That means maybe 10,000 customers are taken, but with over 1 billion people who speak English around the world,¹ that still leaves you 999,990,000 potential clients.

For example, there are lots of website design and e-commerce usability experts online already. But I found a niche that other services hadn't filled yet—*personalized website review videos.* To test this, I bought a descriptive domain name and posted a one page website at www.ExpertWebSiteReviews.com. With no advertising I now get a steady stream of $129 orders from people looking for my opinion on their websites. I record myself and the screen while reviewing their site usability, product strategy, and SEO, then post the personalized, 15-minute review videos to YouTube. The customers love the customized expert feedback and I enjoy both making the videos to help people and the fun income stream the service has created.

The key to this little success story? *Personalization.* There are thousands of qualified website usability and user interface designers and tons of e-books, real books, blogs, and videos about how to best design websites "in theory." But beyond that general advice, real people always want more specific answers to their own specific questions. If you turn your general expertise into specific, personalized solutions, you're more likely to find paying customers, too.

Stop Worrying About Your Credentials

Here's an example of how everyday experience can make a regular guy an "expert":

Octavio had an idea for an online business. His passion is natural healthcare but he was afraid. He felt a calling to share with the world the natural remedies and healthcare products that had helped him feel better because they were not well publicized or appreciated by medical doctors.

His concern? Octavio was worried that no one would believe him because he was not a medical "expert." Luckily, he booked a Private Coaching Call session with me to talk about it. In speaking with him, I learned that Octavio had been working in the vitamins and supplements business for years. Although he doesn't have a medical degree, his personal experience with the topic and his obvious passion for it easily qualify him as a potential expert online.

The dose of confidence that our phone call gave him, plus the support and advice from his fellow ClickMillionaires.com members, encouraged him to finally take action on his dream. His natural supplements website is on its way to attracting a big audience from baby boomers who are increasingly interested in healthy aging strategies.

Join the New Breed of Experts Online

I coach people like Octavio all the time who want to start lifestyle businesses based on their expertise. They are worried no one will take them seriously because they don't have a bunch of initials after their names. Even doctors and lawyers I speak to worry about this.

Traditionally "experts" were those with credentials—Ph.D., M.D., C.P.A., J.D., etc.—but the Web has opened millions of smaller niches where there are no academic credentials available.

You don't have to have a Ph.D. to give good advice. Nobody has a degree in how to buy cheap car insurance or how to attract Facebook followers. Who can bring together the members of your church, help multiple sclerosis sufferers find support, or teach guinea pig breeders to win more blue ribbons at the State Fair? *You!* The growing markets for this kind of niche information and relationships open the door for you to establish yourself as whomever and whatever you want to be. All you need to know is more than your audience so you can help people.

Your Intellectual Property Makes You an Expert

"Am I qualified?" is a question that far too many new entrepreneurs just like Octavio worry about in the middle of the night. The answer, in most cases, is yes, because your *personal intellectual property* makes you an expert. "Intellectual property" is a legal term that usually refers to complex, valuable ideas that are the result of years of study, research, and work. Examples are patents, software code, and books. But you have a unique set of experiences and opinions that constitute valuable intellectual property, too. And today you can use the Internet to position yourself as a leading expert on any topic based on the personal intellectual property that you've developed by simply living your life! Your day-to-day routines, plus whatever you studied in school or learned on the job, add up to lots of specialized knowledge and expertise.

Even the simple act of finding and packaging information and bringing it to your audience can be very valuable. Who has time to dig for info these days? Your target customers are likely busy working and raising their families, so the more info you can easily bring them the more likely they are to appreciate your service, to return, and to tell their friends.

Many people respond even more to the fact that you care about them and are interested in helping. Today you can use social media to offer that help and build those relationships on a more scalable, potentially profitable basis than ever before.

The bottom line is that customers want solutions to their problems. If you've spent hundreds, or even thousands of hours learning how to do something well, there will be plenty of people willing to pay for the shortcuts that your new business can share with them online. Your biography or even the details of your product matter little if your website helps visitors solve their problems.

All this demonstrates that being an "expert" is really a matter of perception. *If the audience believes you know more than they do, you are an expert, at least to them.* And even if you don't know "more," if they like and trust you, then they can be guided by you as a fellow traveler in search of the same goals.

Four Types of Click Millionaire Experts

I see four types of experts online today. Any or all of these may apply to you.

1. *TRADITIONAL EXPERT.* A doctor, lawyer, engineer, etc. Someone with traditional academic credentials and recognized professional standing. Congratulations if you already have these credentials, but if you don't it can be hard (and expensive) to catch up.

2. *NICHE EXPERT.* Here you have experience but in a field that isn't recognized. Maybe you grew up working on old cars, or have traveled a lot, or know every line of dialogue from the *Star Wars*

movies. These "credentials" make you a real expert but only in a narrow area.

3. *JUST-IN-TIME EXPERT*. You are well-informed about a topic but are fairly new to it. You become more of an expert each time you figure out or research the solution to a new problem in that field. For example, you've recently remodeled a house, home-schooled your two children, or had a medical emergency that has changed your life. You are more of an expert than most folks but not yet a "black belt" because you're still learning as you go. I call this a "just-in-time expert" because you are basically just two or three steps ahead of your audience in your expertise level. That relative difference in experience is enough to give you credibility as an expert, at least to beginners. Of course, it helps your credibility if you've earned your knowledge by succeeding at whatever it is you are "experting" about.

4. *CO-LEARNING EXPERT*. You don't have to be an expert at all when you start today. "Sharing the journey" is a legitimate approach even for expertise-based businesses. This is because the Net allows such easy, free, and rapid communication that you can position yourself as exploring a new field *with* your audience. This is a great place to start as a new entrepreneur because you can build credibility with your audience as you explore a new field together. As a co-learning expert you take reader questions, maybe participate in a forum, and make a point of sharing what you learn as you go along. Your very lack of experience can be used as a friendly selling point because you are "in it together" with your audience. For example, it's an increasingly popular approach online to blog about something as you learn it. That positions you as a smart person who is open and honest but more like a *trusted friend* than an expert. As you go along exploring your new field and sharing your knowledge with your audience, you'll become more confident. At first you'll be just one step ahead of your audience in expertise, then two steps, then three. Pretty soon your continued focus on the topic will help you really become an expert rather than just a co-learner. Dedicated focus is all that differentiates any of us from experts in other fields; with all the information available online becoming an expert can happen faster than ever before.

The co-learning expert strategy also works well when interviewing other experts. You can ask them the questions you and your audience want answered. Do that enough times and soon you'll be able to answer the questions yourself! (Or write the e-book, do the radio interview, etc.—just like a "real" expert.)

When you succeed at becoming a Co-Learning Expert, you will soon evolve into a Just-in-Time Expert, and then to a Niche Expert. If you pick an interest and work to build up your expertise through the levels above, your expertise won't be in question for long.

The Easy Way to Become an Expert

As you can see, being an expert is all about perception. If you have a degree from Stanford you are automatically perceived to be an expert in whatever subject your degree is in, even if you spent most of your time in school snowboarding. It's the same way online; if you demonstrate expertise and provide some credentials, people are trained to believe that you are an expert. How do you gain credentials online today? Publish!

Publishing content related to your chosen field is the quickest way to gain online recognition for any expertise. Even without that Stanford degree you can start reading tons of free info on any topic online. If you absorb that information and publish articles, blog posts, videos, or podcasts based on your new knowledge, you can quickly be seen as an authority in your new field, at least relative to people who are newer to the topic then you are.

Bonus? The search engines love authoritative content, too. So if you start publishing consistently and include the key words that the search engines value for your content, the search engine spiders will soon pick up your website to include it in their search results on your chosen topics. This can lead to additional website traffic as people you've never met search online for answers to their problems in your niche. If you provide enough content targeted to their needs (and especially if those visitors share your content online via social networks and other websites start linking back to your content), both the people and the search engines will start treating you like an expert.

> **CLICK MILLIONAIRES SECRET: The Halo Effect**
>
> To paraphrase Wikipedia, the "halo effect" is a cognitive bias whereby the perception of one characteristic of a person or object is influenced by the perception of another trait of that person or object. An example would be judging a good-looking person as more intelligent.
>
> You can put the halo effect to work in your business by appointing yourself the "Editor-in-Chief" or the "Publisher" of your new website's content. Surround yourself with relevant content, present yourself professionally, and the halo of that good content plus your impressive title will present you as an expert to anyone who finds your site, even if you are only five minutes ahead of them in learning about the subject!

They're Not Looking at You Anyway

Many new online entrepreneurs act like one of my aunts did at a recent family wedding. She spent so much time getting dressed and worrying about how she looked that she was late to the ceremony. She almost missed the wedding entirely because she forgot that everyone was there to see the bride, not her. Don't make the same mistake—you are not the bride on your website, your product is. In other words, you don't need to worry so much about impressing your visitors with your credentials because people are much more interested in solving their problems than investigating you.

Visitors have come to your website looking for help in finding a date, learning how to cure their back pain, finding good deals on new furniture, or how to take better care of their pets or houseplants. Notice that little of that has anything to do with you, what you look like, where you went to school, or who your parents are. The fact is that your biography and even your product are only a small part of the evaluation process that each website visitor goes through when deciding whether to purchase from you or not. Customers' real focus is usually 70 percent or more on finding the best solution to his or her problem. Sometimes "best" means cheapest, sometimes it means fastest, sometimes it means most prestigious—it's up to you how you differentiate your offerings. Of customers' remaining attention, most of it—say 20 percent—is focused on evaluating whether the remaining aspects of the product will meet their needs.

That leaves only 10 percent or less of the focus on you. All you need to do is have a professional-looking website and be credible enough yourself so that you do not distract from the purchase process the customer has already decided to enter. If your product is credible, your website is credible. Your credibility derives from that, not the other way around.

Your "About Us" Page Is Critical

To establish credibility today it's very important to have a complete "About Us" page on your website.

This page needs to offer:

▸ A quick summary of your services and the value you provide.

▸ A short mission statement or explanation of why you are in this business.

▸ Email and other contact information.

▸ And, yes, photos of you (and of your team if you have one).

These details are important for visitors to see because they give your anonymous, faceless website a personality, establishing you as a real person and your business as a real thing. They want reassurance that they are not handing over their credit card numbers to a scammer hiding behind a keyboard somewhere. Just like you, they want to deal with a human who looks like somebody they could like and trust. A simple smiling photo of you can go a long way in helping potential customers feel comfortable doing business with you and trusting your site.

Should I Make My Name and Face Part of My Website Brand?

Many websites use an individual as a "spokesperson" to help brand their offerings. But what if you don't want to post your photo or make yourself the center of attention?

A ClickMillionaires.com member wrote to ask me that very question:

Dear Scott,

I'm excited about my new website business, but do I need to use my photo and real name to promote it?

Kathy
Pasadena, California

I answered her as follows:

Hi Kathy,

If you are an individual entrepreneur, you need to brand your business with a face and a name. A face is one of the most memorable things you can display on a web site. Making eye contact, even if it's only with a photo, is light years more powerful for building rapport than even the coolest logo. So, a face will be one of the easiest (and cheapest) ways to differentiate your business online, especially if your site is new. While a group or company may not want to promote one individual as the face of its brand, most customers would still like to see a picture of the founder or the team on the website.

If you don't want to use your own photo, you can use stock photos or even hire a model to "play you" online. This can lead to confusion and will cost you real money over time for more photos, however, so your own picture is better. Your own photo will be cheaper and easier to update over time, plus it's the truth.

For your name, there are different levels of "you" that you can choose to share online. For example, you might be concerned about privacy, about conflicts between your new Click Millionaire business and your "real" job, or even simply that your name is difficult to spell or pronounce. For business purposes online you can call yourself whatever is appropriate for your brand and convenient for you, as long as it is not deceptive or illegal and you are consistent about its usage. Try shortening your name, using a nickname, your middle or maiden name, or even making up a "stage name" for use online. "Betty Crocker" is one of the biggest brands ever but that personality is an advertising creation, not a real person.

All my best for your success,

Scott Fox

How to Fail at Looking Like an Expert

While looking like an expert is easier than ever online, there are still lots of people who are doing it wrong.

Here are the Top 10 Mistakes to Avoid when building your "expert" website:

1. Using an unbranded, free website: Please invest the $10/year to get your own domain name if you want anybody to take you seriously.

2. Broken links and unfinished pages on your website.

3. Using an AOL, Hotmail, or shared email address like susanandpaul@comcast.com.

4. All text with no graphics or photos or logo.

5. A bad headshot, a black-and-white headshot, or no headshot.

6. Music, video, or voices that play automatically.

7. Writing in the future tense: Talking about "what this site is going to be about" or "I plan on . . ." This is not happening "someday," you are making this happen right now.

8. Not collecting email addresses from your visitors.

9. Not having at least a minimum presence on Facebook, Twitter, and LinkedIn.

10. A copyright notice that is out of date.

BONUS #11: *Not making it really obvious how people can contact you and give you money.*

Avoid these simple mistakes and your Click Millionaire lifestyle business will thank you by making more money!

CHAPTER 6 NOTE
1. www.internetworldstats.com/stats7.htm

7

the amazing 10-step click millionaires expert program

IT'S EASY TO over think a new business. Rather than surrendering to Analysis Paralysis, how about taking action instead?

Here's a "quick-start guide" to 10 easy and cheap steps you can take to position yourself as an expert in anything in just 30 days, even in fields you know little about. This guide can help you start your own lifestyle business empire online.

1. Identify a niche industry, interest, or community where you have both expertise and interest.

2. Brainstorm and buy a domain name that includes keywords important to your niche, *and* is cool-sounding, easy to

spell, and memorable. (My InternetMillionaireDomains
.com offers good prices on domain names and I donate the
profits to charity.)

3. Set up a blog. You can use Weebly.com, Blogger.com, or
Wordpress.com for free. Be sure to buy and use a domain
name of your own to look professional, though.

4. Make up a username that matches your domain name and
encapsulates your expert branding. Use it to set up free
accounts on Facebook, Twitter, Google+, and LinkedIn.

5. Set up free Google Alerts. This free search tool from Google
(www.GoogleAlertsTool.com) will scour the Internet nightly
for mentions of any keywords you ask it to seek. Set up these
automated searches to email you daily updates on the top
companies, personalities, products, or issues important to the
people in your target market.

6. Publish on your blog short summaries of the best articles
and blog posts that the Google Alert emails send you each
day. Be sure to link back to the original articles and give
credit where it's due.

7. Demonstrate expertise in your posts and try to help people
in a friendly way on your blog, on your Facebook page, on
Twitter, and on Linked In and Google+, as appropriate for
your topics/industry. Then ask for comments and feedback
to build your brand, traffic, and an audience community.

8. Reach out personally to 20 top people from your industry or
target community. Contact them through email, Facebook,
Google+, or relevant community forums to politely invite
them to read your new blog, participate by leaving comments

and questions, or even submit their own guest posts for you to publish.

9. Set up free accounts with online advertising services like Google AdSense (www.google.com/adsense). Copy and paste the code the system will give you into your new website to create ad banners that pay you each time a visitor to your site clicks on one. (Learn more about profitable pay-per-click and affiliate advertising strategies in Chapter 24.)

10. Repeat steps 6, 7, and 8 to establish yourself as an expert and grow an audience!

Keep publishing and soon your website will start showing up in the search engines. Continue these steps for 30 days and you'll have dozens of blog posts of highly specialized info that is interesting to your target market customers. That will attract visitors who are searching for the same kind of information that your website provides. Publish some more to attract more comments and commentary from your audience, too. As soon as you are ready, start supplementing the content that Google Alerts delivers to you by posting your own original articles, photos, and other content as the "Editor in Chief" of YourNewNicheTopicWebsite.com.

Ta da! Guess who looks like an expert?

While it may scare you to so boldly jump in to building a website and publishing, taking action is exactly what you need to do. Reading books (even good books like mine) won't make you any money. Following this easy plan and the many examples in this book will quickly transform you from a wannabe entrepreneur into an actual online business owner. That shift in mindset is where you want to go if you are going to change your life. Why not start now?

PART THREE

THE BEST INTERNET LIFESTYLE BUSINESSES FOR YOU TODAY

Today's best Click Millionaires lifestyle business systems are explored in the next two parts of the book. Part Three focuses on examples of making money from new products and services that you create, while Part Four shares online business models where you can profit by working for others or promoting their products. These eleven case study chapters discuss how each business system makes money, share profiles of successful entrepreneurs who are making money online with each type of business, and include links to top online vendors for the services needed. They also explain how you can get started replicating these success stories in your own life using the Click Millionaires Lifestyle Business Design Success Principles from Chapter 5.

You don't have to be a genius and find a cure for cancer to become a Click Millionaire. The entrepreneurs in every one of these success stories have simply tweaked existing business models, leveraged Internet tools and distribution, and added their own unique perspective and creativity. You can do this to create a real business for yourself, too.

Warning: Naysayers will argue these ideas have all been done already. But you haven't done your version yet. I have great confidence in you and your ability to create something new, different, exciting, and profitable to upgrade your life.

8

digital publishing is the easiest way to start

THE EASIEST-TO-START business opportunities today let you take advantage of the publishing capabilities of the Internet to attract sales. Fragmented and distracted audiences, piracy, and lower cost competitors are destroying the 20th-century media elite of top newspapers, TV programs, radio stations, record labels, and film studios. There's room for you as one of those lower cost competitors, too.

The next few chapters detail modern publishing ventures for you to consider including:

▸ email newsletters ("noozles")

▸ blogs

› podcasts

› video webcast shows

› online promotions businesses

These are all opportunities for you to step in and grab your piece of the media business by publishing your own digital information. If you pick a profitable target market and serve that audience consistently with content it finds valuable or entertaining, you can make good money with low overhead, and have fun doing it, too.

Digital Magazine Publishing

You can create a "digital magazine" for almost any topic, industry, or subculture today because the Internet has eliminated much of the expense of publishing, removed the geographic boundaries to communications, and allowed previously fragmented groups to be cost-effectively collected into valuable audiences online. Every industry, hobby, sport, religion, or community subculture has its own news, events, gossip, humor, and business opportunities that may offer you profit potential as an online publisher. Click Millionaire businesses based on packaging and redistributing that information are valuable to such communities. Whether you choose to deliver your digital magazine as a newsletter, blog, podcast, video series, or some other new delivery style, your goal is to collect interesting and valuable information and publish it to attract an audience and advertisers.

Traditionally this kind of business need was served by specialized print magazines. But today the free distribution tools of the Internet mean that collecting and sharing the latest news from a particular scene or industry can make money for you—without all of the expensive typesetting, printing, postage, and staff costs of a traditional magazine. By starting an electronic publication like this, you also become a "publisher," automatically positioning yourself as a valued expert in your target market. Traditionally the publisher of a magazine was someone who commanded a big staff and had a large audience. But today you can call yourself a "publisher" even though you're just working from your kitchen table with a laptop after hours. And, once you're in business as a publisher, you can begin attracting the audience, interviews, and advertising revenues that publishers have traditionally commanded.

How Digital Publishers Make Money Online

The business model for most digital publishing is advertising-based. You publish material online to attract as many readers/viewers/listeners as possible. If you collect an attractive audience, advertisers pay you to promote their products. The Internet also makes it easy to sell things online so many Click Millionaire publishers also sell their own e-books or physical products, too.

One of the best parts about this business approach is that much of the content you publish can be obtained for free. As discussed in more detail in Chapter 23, Easy Content Publishing Strategies, your online magazine might include:

› Links to interesting blog posts written by others.

› Repurposed press releases from relevant companies.

› Short summaries of news stories published by others.

› Guest posts from experts, industry executives, or advertisers.

› Photos sent in by your audience.

› Birthday wishes to relevant celebrities, VIPs, or top readers.

› Event listings or job openings.

Your digital publishing business doesn't have to be all business either; it can even include fun general-purpose content like jokes, trivia questions, and links to funny videos.

A "Filter Business" Can Help Your Audience Survive Information Saturation

A proven way to make money is to solve customer problems. One of the biggest problems we all face today is being overwhelmed by the flow of information. Text messages, voice mail, and emails all compete for our daily attention. An interesting new magazine arrives several times a week. Each month I see a couple of new business books that are tempting to read. My DVR is capturing more TV shows right now than I have time to watch (okay, most of those are fun rather than strictly business). There are at least a dozen podcasts and YouTube channels I'd like to follow more closely. Oh, and all those webinars and free teleseminars, too. And, of course don't forget the blogs. Every day I wake up to dozens of relevant and potentially valuable new posts, even though I try hard to narrow my blog diet down to the ones that are most directly applicable to my businesses.

Does this sound familiar to you? This "information saturation" is the same dilemma facing your audience!

People everywhere would like less information to consume. So if your digital magazine can act as an online "filter" that summarizes the latest news specifically for their niche interests, you give them the massive gift of more time for themselves.

Traditionally the nightly news broadcasts on the major networks served this function. The news teams at the networks scoured the world for the most important and most interesting news each day and packaged it into an easy-to-consume half-hour show each night.

Today your online business can serve a similar filtering function for your targeted audience. Like an air filter, an oil filter, or a coffee filter, your "information filter" business can help separate the good stuff from the bad, leaving high-quality air, oil, coffee or in this case news and information for the user. Weed out the fluff, spam, and nonsense to help them keep up with the latest niche news more easily. The value comes both from the work you do in collecting the info into one place and also in the editorial choices you make in filtering the info to provide the most useful bits to your readers.

This may sound too simple but most of us are busier than we want to be these days. Just gathering publicly available information into one place, in an easily accessed and regularly published email newsletter (a "noozle"; see Chapter 9), blog, podcast, video show, e-book, or other digital publication can be a valuable tool to help your audience use its time better, improving their lives.

Starting as the editor of a simple "filter" business that curates the news produced by others is the quickest way to start a digital publication business. If you want to advance beyond that, the usual next step in adding value for your audience is to create original content yourself. You'll find that it's easy to pay others to collect and filter or even write those original articles for you, too.

Digital publishing businesses are among my favorite business systems because they offer you the opportunity to build a business that's not dependent on your personal daily participation. In other words, digital publishing ventures take advantage of Click Millionaires Success Principle #6; they are very scalable. Plus, in just a few weeks of daily publishing on your chosen topic, you will start to appear to be, and then become, the expert you wanted to be.

Can you see the Click Millionaires business system emerging here?

How About a Digital Magazine Based on Your Experience?

Perhaps you have experience in the advertising, nursing, livestock, or catering industries. Or you worked for a big company like Disney,

GM, Enterprise Rent-a-Car, or Fedex. Or you're a Mormon, a social worker, a huge fan of tropical fish, a former fighter pilot, or a fanatic needlepointer. Try creating a blog, email newsletter, video series, or podcast that highlights the latest news and achievements of people like you, and throw in a dose of gossip and photos from related conferences and parties. That approach will quickly create an online magazine that almost anyone in your target market would enjoy reading, especially if you make it easy for them to consume by posting it online or delivering it directly into their email inboxes. If you can find an industry or entertainment niche that has not already been filled, the audience you target may actually be so grateful for your new publication that they see your work as a public service. This is great brand positioning that naturally leads to repeat readership and word-of-mouth growth. And, where there are audience eyeballs, there are also advertising dollars from advertisers who want to reach your target market.

> **CLICK MILLIONAIRES SECRET: Digital Publishing Is a Lifestyle Design Tool**
> One of the exciting parts about digital publishing strategies is that you can use it to begin choosing your own world: You don't have to blog only about topics you already know. Publishing online is so inexpensive that you can start a new blog, podcast, or video series covering issues, people, subjects or products that you would like to learn about. Once you start covering them, you will naturally start interacting with those folks and create opportunities to redesign your life!

Two Types of Click Millionaires Digital Publishing Strategies

There are two types of audiences that you can target with digital publishing: business and consumer. Both offer good opportunities, so let your personal expertise and interests help you choose.

BUSINESS-TO-BUSINESS (B2B) TRADE PUBLICATIONS

My favorite target markets for digital publishing today are business audiences. Even the most old-fashioned industries are now staffed by people who spend time online after work, even if they don't during their shifts. While most of the obvious publishing opportunities are now taken (there are plenty of blogs and newsletters already targeting young male computer programmers), digital publishing niches continue to exist for you in almost any industry.

I think that publishing for business audiences is easier than for consumers today for two reasons:

▸ B2B audiences share business interests. That implies budgets that you can tap by helping them advertise to each other and by selling them your products.

▸ Specialized industry knowledge or connections helps reduce competition.

BUSINESS-TO-CONSUMER (B2C) ENTERTAINMENT AND CONSUMER PUBLICATIONS

There is also always room for more lifestyle, entertainment, hobby, and shopping news. A world full of different opinions about what's important in celebrity gossip, diets, sex, sports, politics, movies, music, hang-gliding, chicken breeding, bonsai gardening, whale watching, and boat maintenance all mean a million micro-audiences are now emerging that you can tap.

There are lots of great examples of entertainment or consumer-targeted noozles thriving online. And they may be more fun to produce—an important Click Millionaire lifestyle benefit!

The following chapter presents case studies of both B2B and B2C email newsletters to help you decide if an email-based digital publishing business model could be your winning Click Millionaire business system.

9

publishing profitable email "noozles"

Although email is often overlooked in favor of sexier new tools, it's still very effective at reaching customers. Social media platforms come and go but email is still the workhorse of the modern economy. You can use old-fashioned email newsletters to create modern lifestyle business successes, too.

What Is a "Noozle"?

"Free email newsletters" is an inconvenient mouthful, especially if it's one you repeat every time you discuss your business. In my last book, *e-Riches 2.0*, I coined the term "noozle" to replace this mouthful. A "noozle" is a free informational newsletter delivered by email for business purposes. If you work with email publishing as much as I do, you'll soon find this phrase useful, too!

It's also worth noting that I'm not talking about emails that are used to promote other products. Noozles are custom-produced email newsletters full of information that *is* the product. Publishing and distributing an email noozle is cheap and easy. Even if you're not at all techie, you probably know how to use email. That helps make noozles a great business approach for non-techie entrepreneurs. As a noozle publisher you can make money either by selling ads or by offering paid subscriptions (And you can do both simultaneously by offering free teasers with paid upgrades, too.)

Publishing a Business-to-Business Noozle

Meet Al Peterson, the publisher of NTS Media Online. His B2B Click Millionaire noozle strategy has helped him graduate from being one of thousands of employees at a multinational publishing firm to being his own boss, publishing a noozle about an industry he loves, and working from his home outside of San Diego, California. Al's noozle business is a trade publication focused on the talk radio business. (The "NTS" in his noozle's name stands for "News, Talk, Sports," his noozle's industry targets.) His daily noozles each contain between four and eight short articles summarizing the latest news in his industry. This news ranges from updates on the day's industry headlines to the latest executive hirings and firings, news of industry controversies or radio station promotions, and pictures of readers at industry events.

Al has decades of radio industry experience, including 11 years as the News, Talk, Sports Radio section editor for the *Radio & Records* trade magazine. When he left R&R in 2008 he drew upon his radio business expertise and relationships to start his own online publication offering business information to the same industry. He has just one partner who handles ad sales and no staff except free-lance contractors who are spread across the country. In just a few years Al has turned his daily emails into a top advertising resource for sponsors who want to reach his exclusive audience of radio station executives, programmers, salespeople, and talk show industry personnel. Subscribing to his emails is free, but he benefits from recurring revenue from the same kinds of sponsors who used to advertise in radio industry magazines.

(In fact, Al has made the transition to the Internet age far better than his previous employers: although *Radio & Records* was an important trade magazine for decades, it was merged into *Billboard* magazine in 2006 and was shut down entirely in 2009.)

CLICK MILLIONAIRE INTERVIEW:
Al Peterson, Publisher/Editor-in-Chief of NTS Media Online

Scott: Al, why did you start NTS Media Online?

Al: I love the radio business. I especially love the news and talk radio business and the people in it. But I had a different vision of the future than my employer did. Digital delivery of industry news seemed like the future to me. I realized that email was the preferred way for people to receive their news these days and it has a lot less overhead than print. I wanted to take my industry knowledge and contacts and translate that to electronic publishing.

Scott: And has that worked out for you?

Al: Yes. Since we started in 2008 our daily email audience has grown to reach almost 100 percent of the top radio stations in the top 100 U.S. radio markets. Our subscribers are the decision makers in talk radio and our advertisers like that.

Scott: You chose to focus on email over building a fancy website. Why is that?

Al: I prefer to put our news under your nose quickly and easily. Email does that nicely. Our website is only a backup to the convenient delivery of email.

Scott: What do you see as the key to success in publishing a noozle like yours?

Al: The biggest difficulty in establishing an email publication is to know who your constituency is and how to reach them before you get the product together. If you know who it is you want to reach and you know how to reach those individuals, then you do your research first to find out what they want. Then you design your product to be what they told you they want. Then you can go back and tell them, "I've got what you want." Usually it works pretty well that way. It has certainly worked for me.

Scott: Do you think there's room for my readers to start their own noozles in other industries today?

Al: Absolutely! I've been talking about talk radio but I think you could do what I do talking about widgets if that's the particular group you're in.

Scott: What do you like best about your business today?

Al: My wife calls this business "the greatest thing that ever happened to me" because I finally figured out how to get people to pay me for my opinions! Over the years I've worked for companies and I've worked on my own. I've just come to learn that I'm always happiest in an environment where I'm calling the shots. I prefer to succeed or fail on my own merits, not on the decisions of someone else that I may or may not agree with.

Scott: What's your advice for readers considering a similar noozle path?

Al: I would recommend that anyone who has entrepreneurial spirit go out there and try it. Give yourself a budget and give yourself a reasonable amount of time to succeed. If you've got the right attitude and you've got the right spirit, you can take a new business from your dining room table to an office conference room table.

The success of his business also allows Al to have some fun as a "big shot" in his industry. He even hosts his own annual "Talk Media Summit" conference each year in Los Angeles, where many of his subscribers pay to attend. It attracts the stars of his industry like Dave Ramsey and Glenn Beck and is another source of revenue.

I chose Al's noozle as our first example of a Click Millionaire business system because it demonstrates how you, too, could:

▸ Leverage experience, training, and connections from your corporate jobs to go solo.

▸ Replace traditional print magazine printing and mailing costs with free online distribution to keep costs down.

▸ Target a niche of valuable subscribers clustered around a common business interest.

▸ Deliver timely, topical information that helps your readers do their jobs better.

To succeed as a noozle publisher you don't need Al's decades of experience in your target market, nor do you need to create all new content daily yourself like he does. (Of course outsourcing his article writing would increase his overhead costs but it would also free up his time—a lifestyle choice that is Al's to make.) While Al's experience and relationships certainly helped him build his business, today you can more quickly get started as a noozle publisher in any target market using Chapter 7's "Amazing 10-Step Click Millionaires Expert Program."

Other examples of successful B2B noozles that I recommend you look at include business-oriented publications like:

- Ned Sherman's Digital Media Wire (www.digitalmediawire .com—profiled in more detail in both of my previous books).

- Ben Kuo's SoCalTech (covering the venture capital industry in Southern California—www.socaltech.com).

- Seth Godin's visionary marketing and management insights (www.sethgodin.com)

- Bob Lefsetz's irascible music industry commentary (www.lefsetz.com).

- John Kremer's book marketing advice at www.bookmarket.com.

- Andy Sernovitz's clever marketing tips at www.damniwish.com

- Rich Galen's inside the Beltway political commentary (www.mullings.com).

- Henry Blodget's Business Insider top business news stories from www.businessinsider.com.

Publishing a Consumer Noozle

While the consumer market may be more crowded than B2B markets, there is always room for entertaining, informative, or useful new noozles that offer a unique service or fun point of view.

CLICK MILLIONAIRE PROFILE:
Randy Cassingham, Founder, This is True

Randy Cassingham figured out there was a consumer market for newsletters before almost anyone else. In fact, for years Randy thought he had *invented* for-profit email publishing—at least until one older newsletter turned up. He started publishing his noozle, *This is True*, while work working at NASA's Jet Propulsion Laboratory in Pasadena, California way back in 1994. This means he was on the Internet even before I was!

Randy wanted to be a syndicated newspaper columnist but those opportunities were few. Soon the Internet came to his rescue. Randy tells the story like this:

> For years, I had posted weird-but-true newspaper clippings on a bulletin board outside my cubicle at the Jet Propulsion Laboratory. Just posting clippings wasn't enough: I couldn't help but write comments on the articles. For instance, one that I recall was about a woman who kept two things under her pillow: an asthma inhaler . . . and a gun. One night she had an asthma attack, grabbed the gun instead of the inhaler, stuck it in her mouth, and pulled the trigger. On the article I wrote, "There she goes, shooting her mouth off again."
>
> As the years went by, the clippings (and my commentary) got very popular at JPL. I'd just call out "New clips going up!" and go sit down, and clusters of people would crowd around the bulletin board in the hallway to catch the news—and laugh at the comments.

In 1994 Randy realized that this demand could probably help him build a business online. Since then his *This is True* noozle has attracted almost 50,000 subscribers from 200+ countries. Why? They love the funny news stories Randy finds for them. He collects stories of stupid criminals, inept teachers, drunken idiots, and strange behavior from all over the world. He summarizes them and adds his own humorous or ironic comments to create unique and entertaining content for free. Randy says that because of his early start as an email newsletter publisher he was also one of the first people in the world to quit his full-time job to become an Internet entrepreneur, way back in 1996. He left crowded Los Angeles and now he and his Colorado-native wife live in rural Western Colorado in a 550-sq-mile county of only 4,100 people and one traffic light.

Today Randy's email publishing empire makes money from both advertising and from paid subscriptions. The free version of his noozle (www.thisistrue.com) contains ads paid for by sponsors, and premium subscribers pay $24/year for more stories and no ads. Today he manages *This is True*, and has also expanded into similar online publishing ventures like Jumbo Joke, Cranky Customer, and a site about outrageous-but-true lawsuits, too, plus a million-selling line of cards, stickers, and other merchandise at GetOutOfHellFree.com.

This winning Click Millionaires approach can be applied to your interests, too. Especially if you have a good sense of humor or another unique twist to differentiate your noozle, almost any topic can be mined for the recurring revenues that Click Millionaires seek.

For example, AllHipHop's urban music news, Joyce Showalter's inspiring Heroic Stories, Daily Candy's shopping and fashion tips noozle (which was purchased by Comcast for $125 Million!), Thrillist's rapid growth to a $40MM+ year /business, and even the multi-billion dollar success story of Groupon is based on the simple noozle publishing model of inexpensive emails offering short bits of consumer-targeted content.

How You Can Make Money with Noozles

As demonstrated by Al and Randy's success, advertising is the most common way to make money from noozles. Most noozles are distributed for free. This is to attract readers and help your audience grow virally as readers forward your new publication to their friends. Profitable advertising can be a challenge when you have few subscribers. But if your noozle targets a valuable demographic, especially an industry where people have and spend money, you'll likely begin being able to attract advertisers with just a few hundred subscribers.

You may also be able to charge for subscriptions if your noozle is really good, but in today's competitive online publishing race, that's more likely a "phase two" step for after you've established a strong free readership and you've also sold some "upgrades" to your free service to test the loyalty of your readers.

How to Start Your Noozle Business

The tools you need to start an email newsletter business are well established and available inexpensively from many providers. To get going you just need an account with an email service provider like AWeber, Constant Contact, FeedBlitz, Mailchimp, iContact, or any of their many competitors. These companies usually offer free trials to get started and service fees of $20–$30 per month for small mailing lists. For this monthly fee you get a fully managed, corporate-grade email subscriber system for sending your emails. You will also be provided with the snippets of HTML code that you need to paste onto your website in order to collect email addresses. These services will then add new subscriber addresses to your account's online database, help people unsubscribe, and send out your emails with preferred delivery from the top Internet service providers (ISPs). (This last part is important to help your noozles avoid being labeled as spam.)

You can start even cheaper by sending your noozles from your personal email account, but I recommend using a professional email services provider instead. Any new noozle email list will likely begin with you simply collecting the email addresses of your friends and family, but personally managing your list is not a good use of your time. For example, it quickly becomes awkward when people start subscribing and unsubscribing constantly. And, most ISPs will block your email as spam if they see you blasting out hundreds or thousands of emails from a personal account.

Noozles vs. Blogs—Which Is Better?

Today the most popular way to regularly publish short bits of information online is by blogging. Both blogs and email noozles usually offer similar collections of short articles, so the big question is which is more convenient for your audience? Your goal is to attract readers so that you can make some money. To do that you want to serve content up in the ways that your audience is most likely to read and share it.

Email is still my favorite format because it is the most convenient for readers. Visiting your blog regularly requires them to take extra time out of their busy day. But email newsletters arrive right in their email inboxes automatically. That makes it really easy for them to read (and see your ads). Especially for business audiences the email inbox is where work gets done and where most attention is focused.

ClickMillionaires.com Member Bonus: If you would like to put the best of both blogs and noozles to work marketing your business online, visit ClickMillionaires.com for a free video walk-through. I'll show you step-by-step how to set up a clever and affordable service that will republish your blog posts as email newsletters automatically!

10

blogging to the bank

BLOGGERS MAKE money by publishing to niche audiences that could never have afforded to have had their own magazines in the days of newspapers and print magazines.

What Is a Blog?

A blog is just a type of website that features regularly updated short articles—another type of "digital magazine." The articles are posted chronologically (most recent first) and cluster their topics around a niche interest of the blog's owner/author. Blogs (short for "weblogs") started as personal diaries for techies looking to share their daily musings with their friends. They have evolved into a big industry now as their powerful publishing capabilities have helped them explode in popularity. Today anyone can quickly and easily start a blog to share his or her thoughts with the world. As an online entrepreneur you can use a blog as a publishing tool to not only share your thoughts online but to create a niche magazine-style business of your own.

Contributing to their popularity, blogs also enjoy several key features that traditional newspapers and print magazines lack:

> • *Cheap and convenient:* Blogs are cheap and easy to publish and easy and free for readers to access. They can be read on multiple platforms (online via web browsers, on mobile devices, using RSS readers, syndicated as email newsletters, etc.) anytime, 24/7.

> • *Up-to-date:* Most blogs are published at least weekly and many top blogs publish between five and ten (or more) new stories every day.

> • *Interactive:* Blogs improve on the traditional "Letters to the Editor" section of magazines by allowing the audience to comment. This allows quick, easy feedback to the blog authors and the development of reader communities where audience members with similar interests can interact and bond over the blog's content. This can increase traffic, reader loyalty, and the quality of the commentary on the blog, too.

> • *Syndicatable:* All blogs are designed to include "really simple syndication" (RSS) data feeds. This means that the blog's articles are automatically available for easy syndication to other websites, social networks, and online services, thus easily spreading the blog's content and POV to new sites to attract more readers.

Blog Success Stories

Blogs have been around long enough now that the media has reported plenty of success stories:

▸ Graham Hill of Treehugger.com sold his green lifestyles blog for $10MM.

▸ Johns Wu's Bankaholic.com was acquired for $15 million by Bankrate.

▸ AOL bought Jason Calacanis's Weblogs for $25 million, Arianna Huffington's Huffington Post for $315 million, and Michael Arrington's Techcrunch for more than $25 million.

▸ Nikki Finke's Deadline Hollywood was purchased by the Mail Media Corporation for $14 million.

▸ Amit Agarwal of Digital Inspiration has become India's first professional blogger and a columnist for the *Wall Street Journal India*, too.

There are also millions of smaller blogs that are making good money independently by successfully serving niche audiences with information they find entertaining and valuable.

How to Succeed as a Blogger Today

To build an audience as a blogger today, you need to do more than publish articles. You need to serve the needs of a niche audience in a creative way. Click Millionaire Kristin Espinasse's French Word of the Day blog does this nicely.

> *CLICK MILLIONAIRE PROFILE:*
> **Kristin Espinasse of French-Word-a-Day.com**
> Kristin had always dreamed of becoming a writer, but found herself stuck as a secretary at a winery. At least the winery was near

St. Tropez in France where American Kristin had moved after marrying her college sweetheart, a Frenchman. To practice her writing and hopefully develop an audience for her stories, Kristin started a blog. Using her family and local villagers as the cast of characters and the adventures of living in provincial France as her source material, she started publishing stories online under the guise of teaching her audience how to speak French.

She called her blog "French Word a Day" because she discovered that there is an audience of people who want to learn French, speak French better, or just learn about France. By writing entertaining English-language stories about French country life and sprinkling French phrases and pronunciation instructions into them, she attracted these readers to visit her site regularly and subscribe to her blog by email. While Kristin struggled to find time before and after work to publish her stories, she quickly found a small audience who enjoyed her insights to life in Provence and brushing up on their French, too. In fact, her audience was so targeted that she was able to get her first paying sponsors after collecting only 50 subscribers.

She left her job and never looked back. Kristin's stories of life on a working French vineyard, her husband and children (and dog, Smokey), her interactions with the local French villagers, and the intrigue of daily life as told through the eyes of a perceptive foreign observer all combined with her beautiful photographs of the French countryside life to create a niche lifestyle business. Today her French-Word-a-Day.com blog has tens of thousands of subscribers. She makes money from advertising on the site and in her emails, by selling subscriptions to her most loyal fans, and she has published several books of stories collected from her blog posts.

Interestingly, Kristin has built her audience with almost zero marketing or participation in social media. She says "I tried Twitter and Facebook but quit. It just felt 'too markety' for me. But if your readers enjoy what you're doing because you're putting all your time into it, then they will tell their friends about it for you via Facebook and Twitter and all of the 'social stuff'."

I asked Kristin a few questions about blogging and what it's done for her.

Scott: What do you think about your success in building a lifestyle business through blogging?

Kristin: I remind myself just how grateful and lucky I am to be able to do this. Every single experience, even going on vacation, is grist for the mill. It really helps you to appreciate the present moment because it could very well be your next assignment to write about it.

Scott: Do you think there's still room to start new lifestyle businesses by blogging?

Kristin: Oh, definitely, there is so much room. For the person who's passionate, who really wants to live their dream of working for themselves, or of sharing something important, and they want to get paid for it, there's plenty of room. It's good to have fresh voices from people who are new and have new ideas. As cheesy as it sounds, it's like the Nike slogan "just do it!" You have to put yourself to work and just enjoy the fact that you can put all your creativity into it. Just do it with a smile and do it with all your heart and you'll have no problem getting people to sign up.

Scott: Do you think that blogging still offers a valid passport to more fun lifestyle?

Kristin: Definitely. Once you get your creative mind going you can find your own way into it. I can't tell you how strongly I would recommend it. The ability to work for myself doing what I want to do is priceless.

Scott: What would you rather be doing?

Kristin: There's really nothing else I'd rather be doing than to have this chance of writing the next story about some character I've met or about a part of the world I've encountered where there's beauty, where's there's hope, and where's there's something interesting to share with other people. This really is the best. I feel really lucky to be doing exactly what I want to be doing.

Not bad for a lady who failed French in high school, right? Today Kristin finds herself as excited about building lifestyle businesses online as I am. She told me that today she asks anyone who brings up the topic, "Why not start your own business online?"

Kristin's clever system is one you could try, too. Start with a popular topic (like French culture) and find an angle that encourages repeat readership (like offering a "word a day" to learn or another type of helpful tip). In Kristin's case that approach lets readers justify the time they are spending reading her stories and looking at her pretty pictures as "education" because they are advancing their French language skills.

> **CLICK MILLIONAIRES SECRET:**
> **Spice Up Your Blog with Photos**
> As Kristin's success shows, eye-catching imagery is an important part of successful blogging because it attracts and holds reader attention. If you're not a photographer yourself, I recommend iStockPhoto.com for low cost, royalty-free images that you can use to spice up your blog posts visually. You can also search on photo sharing sites like Flickr for free to find millions of Creative Commons–licensed photos that photographers are often willing to share in exchange for photo credits or links.

How to Make Money Blogging

Most blogs make money from advertising displayed on their sites. Then, the more readers they attract, the more money the blogger makes from visitors clicking on the ads. As discussed more in Chapter 24, the most popular advertising service to use is Google's AdSense. By registering for a free account you can copy and paste the AdSense code into your website for free. This will cause ads to start displaying on your blog within minutes, offering you an introductory monetization strategy right away.

Six Quick Steps to Building Your First Blog

A blog is the easiest and fastest online business you can start today. In just minutes you can sign up for a web-based blogging service and start typing to share your thoughts with the world. Here's a quick start guide to getting started:

STEP #1: PICK A BLOG-HOSTING SERVICE. You can use a free or low-cost blogging service like Wordpress, Typepad, Blogger, or Tumblr to create a blog online. (Most blog software today is "hosted" online in a "cloud" of remotely located servers. That means you access your files, content, and software through your Internet browser software (Firefox, Internet Explorer, Chrome, etc.) rather than installing the software on your own computer.) Wordpress is probably the most powerful and popular these days (at least partially because it's free) but it requires regular upgrades and security patches. Typepad is the service I use. It's not free but it is less work to maintain than Wordpress. Blogger is Google's free blog service. Historically Blogger was not as powerful as Wordpress or Typepad but it may be worth considering, especially because Google is likely to integrate its blogs with Google+ and its other services. Most blog services today offer basic functionality similar to these options. Pick one and sign up to create an account and then pick a decorative "theme" for the page design, header image, colors, and fonts.

Cost: Free to $20/month.

STEP #2: CHOOSE YOUR DOMAIN NAME. Pick a domain name that is short, memorable, easy-to-spell, available, and ideally has a .com extension. Adjust the "domain mapping" settings so that the domain becomes the web address for your new blog.

Cost: $10/year or less.

STEP #3: OPTIMIZE TO ATTRACT FREE SEARCH ENGINE TRAFFIC. Identify keywords that search engine users would use when searching for the topics discussed on your new blog. Implement search engine optimization strategies (SEO) by trying to include those keywords in your domain name, page titles, post titles, menu items, file names, and throughout your blog's content. This will help Google and the other search engines recognize what your blog is about and direct searchers to visit you.

Cost: Free.

STEP #4: DEVELOP AN "OFF-SITE" MARKETING PLAN. Consider from the start how your blog content is going to attract readers. You'll want to write about topics that interest your target audience and hopefully help them solve problems, too. The better you get at this, the more your audience will share your blog posts in social media and link back to your site from their own. This will help enhance your search engine rankings further to attract more free traffic because Google counts links back, mentions, likes, and similar social media expressions of approval as evidence that your site's content is valuable for its own search results.

Cost: Free.

STEP #5: INSTALL ADSENSE. Join Google's free pay-per-click advertising program. Copy and paste the code provided into your blog's header, side bars, and/or post templates. That will allow you to start earning money whenever a visitor to your blog clicks on an ad.

Cost: Free.

STEP #6: START COLLECTING EMAIL ADDRESSES. You don't want to be 100 percent dependent on visitors to come find you, you want to be able to market to them also. Building an email list is the best way to do this. Sign up for an email service provider like Aweber, Constant Contact, Feedblitz, or Mailchimp to get the code you need to install on your new blog to collect email addresses from people who visit your website.

Cost: Varies. Most start free and then cost between $10 and $30/month.

These six steps will create a publishing platform for you and position your new blog as a Click Millionaire publishing business system online.

Total start-up cost: *Less than one nice dinner out per month.*

Easy Blog Production Strategies

To get your blog going, start writing short articles, usually between 200 and 600 words each, about whatever topic you like. To increase readership smart bloggers dress up their articles with graphics and also offer their blog posts by email (so that your new articles are delivered automatically to your readers' email inboxes). Publish one short article per month or 10 long articles daily, it's up to you to decide what your target audience wants to read about and how often.

Producing new blog posts constantly can be demanding, so it also helps if you like to write. If writing is not a favored activity for you, here are some alternate blogging strategies to help get your blog going:

- Recruit friends and industry contacts to act as "guest blog-gers" contributing posts for your blog.

- Repost free articles from article banks like EzineArticles.com or other sites you can find by Googling "free articles."

- Interview people or review products to reduce the amount of original content you need to create.

- Try the filtering and linking strategies discussed earlier in Chapter 8.

- Review "An Easy Four-Week Content Publishing Plan," detailed in Chapter 23.

Because starting a blog is so easy there's a lot of competition in the blogosphere. To succeed, use the earlier chapters of this book to be sure you identify a profitable niche and market your content well using the strategies detailed in my previous book, *e-Riches 2.0: Next Generation Online Marketing Strategies*. Or register for Traffic Building School, my email training course that will introduce you to a new Internet marketing tactic each day by sending a short video to your email inbox. Learn more at www.TrafficBuildingSchool.com or by joining us at ClickMillionaires.com.

· · · · · · · 11 · · · · · · ·

making money as
a podcaster and
internet radio star

PODCASTS OFFER a great opportunity to bring audiences together around niche topics. Like our other digital publishing approaches, this means you can make money if you collect an audience that advertisers find attractive, or use the podcasts to promote products of your own.

What's a podcast, you ask? It sounds techie but a podcast is simply a recording. It can be a recording of an Internet-only radio show, a traditional broadcast radio program, a lecture, a phone call, music, or any other audio presentation that listeners can enjoy. Podcasts today are usually distributed in the MP3 file format and downloaded to digital music players like iPods or smartphones for listening. Podcasts can also often be "streamed" online by clicking the "play" button on a webpage that offers an embedded audio player like the one pictured here.

Because the recordings are digital files they can be distributed through the Internet and archived online basically for free. So, although Internet radio shows do not usually have the wide preexisting audiences of traditional radio stations, their MP3 recordings can be shared online for free and they remain available long after the live broadcast is finished.

Most podcasts today are offered primarily as promotional tools. Individuals and companies record and post their shows online to create a publicity platform where they can discuss their products or services.

As our lives become more and more "digital," the podcast audience is growing rapidly. In its earlier years podcasting was dominated by technology-oriented shows targeting the usually young and male computer users who were the primary Internet audience. In recent years more mainstream topics have become the norm, with podcasts about sports, business, health, politics, and comedy attracting large listenership beyond the early adopter tech crowd. This trend is only going to continue because niche audiences want niche entertainment, information, and solutions to their problems. A podcast is a perfect way to deliver this niche information and personalize it with the warmth of your voice speaking directly to your audience, radio-style.

CLICK MILLIONAIRE PROFILE:
Betty in the Sky with a Suitcase

An entrepreneur who shares my excitement about the business potential of podcasting as a Click Millionaire lifestyle business for you is Betty. Betty is probably the world's most popular and famous flight attendant. Why? Because she hosts a podcast that shares entertaining behind-the-scenes stories from the airline industry. This surprising topic (and Betty's fun and funny style) have helped make her "Betty in the Sky with a Suitcase" podcast attract as many as 20,000 listeners per episode. Listeners worldwide tune in for funny stories about mix-ups, mishaps, and misunderstandings on airplane flights. Betty produces the show herself using stories from her 17 years of personal experience, plus pilots, flight attendants, and passengers contribute stories to the broadcasts, too.

I had the pleasure of interviewing her recently.

Scott: Betty, how did you get your podcast started?

Betty: I was always sharing the funny stories that flight attendants tell about the crazy things that happen on airplanes, things that the passengers sitting there never even know about. I like to talk and I'm a bit of a ham. So in 2005 a pilot I was flying with invited me to appear on his podcast. He had a microphone and recording equipment with him on a flight one day, so I went up into the cockpit and told some stories. He encouraged me to give him some more stories for

his show. So I went out and spent $500 on a recorder and a microphone. But I had no idea how to do anything (as you don't when you're new to something) so the audio I sent him was so terrible that he said "Why don't you go do your own show instead"? At that point I had appeared on his show and I had the equipment so I decided I had to try podcasting for myself. Luckily that pilot told his audience to try my show, too, so I had some listeners right away. My podcast has turned a normal life into something that people really like and are interested in, and then turned it into a business, too.

Scott: Did you think that telling stories as a podcaster was going to be a business for you?

Betty: No. It was totally accidental and I didn't know that I was ever going to make any money at it. The amazing thing is that I didn't really do anything except put the podcast out there on the Internet. I didn't try to market it, I didn't do any advertising, and it led to all kinds of other things. Nobody cared about what I had to say until I started broadcasting on the Internet. Once I started podcasting, a publisher contacted me and asked me if I wanted to write a book. Before that nobody was contacting me to offer me book deals. Now whenever there's a new event that involves flight attendants, reporters start calling me because my name and podcast show up highly ranked in Google search results. The BBC, NPR, *Travel & Leisure* magazine, all these major publications and radio stations call to interview me.

Scott: How do you work the podcast production into your busy traveling lifestyle?

Betty: That's another thing that's amazing about the whole podcasting and Internet business thing. Life can happen. You're not trading your hours for wages. You can take a break if something else is going on, like when I took a few weeks off to move.

Scott: Who's listening to your podcast and how many of them are there?

Betty: I just looked recently and it's almost 1,000,000 total downloads—which is crazy! It's been growing over time and now my podcast seems to be getting more popular than it's ever been. I'm currently getting about 20,000 listens per episode.

Scott: How do you find stories?

Betty: I interview people at work and then people just email me stories, I don't even ask, they just want to contribute to the show. People really do like old-fashioned storytelling. Original, personal stories make people start to feel like they know you and you're their friend. My podcasts are basically "in their heads" when they're listening on their iPods.

Scott: It sounds like you have a web-based business, but you haven't spent much time or money on a website. Is that right?

Betty: That's correct. I haven't spent really any. Just $5.00/month for Libsyn.com to host my shows, archive them, and help distribute them. Granted my website should be better and I really should hire someone to do that but it seems to be doing fine without spending a lot of money on it.

Scott: How did you learn the technical details of producing a podcast?

Betty: I have no idea what I'm doing! I basically just learned as I did it. Listeners would write me to point out problems with my audio and then I would Google the problem to teach myself how to fix it. The listeners have really helped with that.

Scott: How are you making money with your podcast?

Betty: I've recently gotten much better at that. What I've realized is that I can just ask on the podcast for the listeners to click on my affiliate ads, like for Amazon.com. I've tried so many different avenues. It's been the best one and it doesn't take any effort on my part except for asking for clicks in 30 seconds on the podcast. People actually want to support my show and they want me to continue doing it. So I think they like doing it, I make a commission off of it, and I don't have to spend any time on it! I just had somebody else contact me about sponsoring the show. If we do that they'll pay me just to mention their company at the beginning of each show. I like that much better than me just relying on the listeners clicking to purchase the product.

Scott: So show sponsorships and affiliate ads are your main revenue sources?

Betty: Yes, but I'm working on turning my podcast into different income streams that continue to grow without necessarily having to put that much more effort into them. So I started a little online store where I sell T-shirts (that costs me just six dollars per month at Cafepress.com). I just get a commission for each sale but I like that because they make the products, they collect the money for it, and they do the shipping. I also wrote a book so I get royalties on that. All those streams of income can keep making you money over time. For example, people go back and listen to old episodes and then they click on my advertising links, too. I like the fact that I don't have to do any of that legwork.

Not everything I've earned is in money, either. I've been real happy. The goodwill that has come about from this podcast is shocking to me. People email me from the hospital and say "I was sick and I found your podcast and it really helped me through the healing process." I think "Really? Who would have thought?" And I'm in the process of writing a second book right now. Which I never thought I'd get to say because I never thought I'd even write a first book! The BBC even called me the world's first podcasting flight attendant. I never thought I'd be the "first in the world" of anything! Now when I have a down day, I love to press my answering machine playback button. I can hear big name radio show producers, NPR, and magazine and newspaper reporters from *USA Today*, *Psychology Today*—we're talking some real publications that like my stuff. I ask myself "Who's life is this? It wasn't mine just a few years ago!"

Scott: What advice do you have for others considering podcasting as a lifestyle business opportunity?

Betty: I can't imagine that whatever you're doing couldn't be helped by having your own podcast. And it's not difficult to do. I know a lot of people look at something like this and think "I could never do that" or "I can't do that" but if I can do it, they can too. I would say most people over the age of 25 don't realize the value of the Internet, how important it is, how far it reaches. Once you put something out there the opportunities that can come back to you are innumerable. The hardest thing is just starting. I only started because that pilot gave me a nudge. But once you put some creative energy and man hours into it you can build a brand and a platform. I did that without even realizing it and now I have many different monetary streams coming from the platform that my podcast's audience has created for me.

My Own Click Millionaires Success Internet Radio Show Example

Like Betty, podcasting is one of the parts of my Click Millionaire lifestyle business that I enjoy the most. My Click Millionaires Success Show has been distributed online since 2008. It's available for free at ClickMillionairesRadio.com and you can also subscribe on iTunes and BlogTalkRadio.com. We also post each episode to my own blogs at ScottFox.com and ClickMillionaires.com, and syndicate the show through Geekcast.FM, Facebook, Twitter, and Google+.

Thousands of people listen to each recording online. The podcasts are a win-win marketing tool: Listeners get valuable information, I get to have fun helping them, and the interesting interviews help attract more listeners and new promotional partners, too.

Podcasting is a strategy I recommend to you, too. It's especially good for those of you who would rather talk than write. You can create good content inexpensively simply by interviewing your friends, authors, and executives from companies that serve your target market.

How You Can Start Your Own Podcast

It may sound complicated to produce a podcast but it's easier than you think. Any microphone or telephone headset that will connect to your computer can be used as an input device to record your voice. Press the red "record" button in a free audio recording tool like Audacity and start speaking. (Audacity is the same free software that Betty uses—you can download it for free at audacity.source-forge.net.) Click to save and you have created a recording. You can then upload that file to your website to offer that recording for free download to visitors. That's all there is to creating a podcast.

Of course, you can spend a lot of money buying professional equipment and spend time worrying about your audio levels, music backgrounds, and production quality. Because podcasts are often listened to in headphones, it's true that audio quality is extra important. But, at the same time, people aren't usually expecting a professional production when they download a podcast. They're looking for the more casual style, unique perspective, and entertainment that you are providing targeted to their niche needs and interests.

So, although Betty spent $500 on her setup equipment, that's just not necessary anymore. You can even start podcasting simply using your telephone and calling in to a free service like BlogTalkRadio.com.

A free basic account there will allow you to record podcasts by phone, including allowing guests to call in for interviews and to ask questions. It also archives your shows, provides embed HTML code that you can use to post a player on your own website for each show, and provides basic statistics about listenership, too. Podcast purists look down on Blog Talk Radio because it's free and easy to use—but I think those are bonuses!

> **CLICK MILLIONAIRES SECRET:**
> **Free iTunes Syndication**
> iTunes offers the world's largest directory of podcasts. Submitting your show to its search engine will help you attract new listeners for free. To get your podcast listed, visit the "Podcast" section on iTunes. Click on the "Submit a Podcast" link on the right-hand side. Paste in the URL of your podcast feed. iTunes will automatically start collecting each episode of your show and archiving it in their directory for iTunes users worldwide to discover, download, and subscribe to for free.

How to Make Money from Podcasting

With podcasts you can make money both indirectly and directly.

To make money indirectly is the easiest. Your podcast can be a great promotional platform for an existing business. You can use your show to promote your products, introduce new products, and interview VIPs who are interesting to your target market. All of this informative activity around your audiences' interests naturally leads to discussion and promotion of products (yours or your advertisers') if you do it right. This can easily lead to more sales, consulting opportunities, speaking gigs, promotional partnerships, and even paid sponsorships.

To make money more directly you can sell ads and sponsorships for your podcast. Unfortunately, so far there is no easy to use free advertising system like Google's AdSense for podcasts (although some podcasting networks do sell ads on their networks and offer revenue shares to their podcasting numbers). So to make money you can install advertising on your website and use your podcast "air time" to ask people to visit your site like Betty does. For more details on how to attract sponsors and their advertising dollars, see Chapter 24, The Secrets of Online Advertising

Benefits of Podcasting

I'm a big fan of podcasting. It's an easy and cheap way to spread your marketing messages and have some fun, too. Other benefits of podcasting include:

- *Making money:* Your podcast is not just a vehicle for your content, it's also a promotional platform for your products and advertisers.

- *Having a creative outlet:* As a podcaster you are the host and star of the show. You get to pick the guests, ask the questions, and set the agenda to make the show as interesting and entertaining as possible for your audience.

- *Meeting interesting people:* As the host of your own "radio show," you can gain access to celebrities, authors, and the VIPs of your industry for interviews.

- *Building relationships:* Hearing your voice regularly builds a sense of a personal relationship with your listeners. This is fun, it builds loyalty, and it encourages free word-of-mouth marketing as your audience tells their friends about your show and products.

- *Enjoying expert status:* By hosting a show dedicated to your niche's topics, you will quickly be perceived as an expert in that field. This offers you a "halo effect" that should help you attract more business as well as speaking, consulting, and event invitations.

‣ *Building a library:* A series of podcasts can quickly grow into a library of shows. This is an asset that can continue to attract listeners and drive traffic to the websites you mention on the air. Betty said, "Radio historically was live. You listen to it and it's gone. But with podcasting it stays there, so once you get a new fan they'll go back and listen to the older episodes, too." Like Betty, I have personally found that this can generate recurring income for you even long after you have finished podcasting.

Betty told me that she "probably wouldn't have gotten started as a podcaster without a nudge" from her pilot friend.

Consider yourself nudged!

CLICK MILLIONAIRES SECRET: The Easy (Free) Way to Get Guests for Your Podcast

One of the challenges for any new podcaster is to find interesting guests to interview. I faced this challenge myself when I started podcasting back in 2008. To solve it I started a free online service called RadioGuestList.com. Now the leading Internet radio and podcast guest interview booking service on the Internet, you can take advantage of RadioGuestList.com, too. As a podcast producer, you can submit "Guest Requests" for free. Use the easy online form to describe the type of guests you are looking for and share some details about your show. RadioGuestList.com will then email your submission to a worldwide audience of thousands of experts, PR firms, authors, and celebrities who are looking for interview opportunities. This free service can save you tons of time and quickly accelerate your podcast toward becoming a profitable Click Millionaire lifestyle business for you.

Other Podcasting Resources

Some podcast shows I enjoy include:

- Mitch Joel's "Six Pixels of Separation" (www.twistimage.com/podcast): A marketing and communications podcast that offers timely insights into modern marketing.

- Andrew Warner's "Mixergy" (mixergy.com): A smart entrepreneur interviews other smart entrepreneurs and company founders for startup wisdom.

- The Smart Passive Income Podcast (www.smartpassive income.com/category/podcast): Goes behind the scenes of Pat Flynn's Internet marketing success story.

- The Big Biz Show (bigbizshow.com): A nationally syndicated "real" daily business talk radio show where I am a regular guest.

- Peter Anthony Holder's "The Stuph File" (peteranthony-holder.com): A fun podcast featuring entertainment and odd news where I've been interviewed several times.

- The Podcast Answer Man (podcastanswerman.com/category/podcastanswerman): Cliff Ravenscraft's show can help you learn to produce your own high quality podcasts.

- Click Millionaires Success Show (www.ClickMillionaires Radio.com): And, don't forget our free episodes that you can listen to anytime online (or download to your smartphone or MP3 player). Entertaining and helpful interviews with experts on Facebook marketing, public relations, PPC advertising, affiliate marketing, and many other proven Click Millionaires success strategies are available online now.

For more examples of popular podcasts (and to check out what's already being broadcast in your niche), visit these sites:

www.iTunes.com/podcasts

www.podcastdirectory.com

www.podcastalley.com

www.podfeed.net

www.stitcher.com

12

your own (web) tv show

VIDEO IS AN increasingly popular business tool online. Whether you produce short clips to promote your products on YouTube, stream live video webcasts using tools like Ustream or Livestream, or do live video chats via Skype or Google+, these tools can help you build a Click Millionaire lifestyle business around your own online video. It's easier than ever before to produce your own "show" for online distribution, and make money doing it, too.

In the United States alone more than 15 billion video streams are now watched every month.[1] In fact, YouTube is the second biggest search engine in the world, more popular than both Bing and Yahoo.

Millions of people are online right now searching for help with niche topics like buying a home, curing dandruff, speaking Swahili, or grooming guinea pigs. This offers major opportunities for you to make money from posting helpful or entertaining videos yourself.

YouTube is the best place for entrepreneurs looking to make money from the massive worldwide audience for online video. The advertising that YouTube runs generates millions of dollars in revenue share annually for the video producers who are members of its "Partners Program." Created in 2007, the Partner Program sells the ads you see on YouTube and passes 60 percent of the revenue back to more than 20,000 video producers from 22 countries. Hundreds of these producers are now making six figures a year or more from their YouTube advertising revenue share and many have quit their jobs to enjoy new lifestyles as video producers, educators, and entertainers online.

CLICK MILLIONAIRE INTERVIEW:
Dave Powers, YouTube Star

Dave Powers is a former personal trainer who has struck it big on YouTube. Believe it or not, he has built a thriving lifestyle business online by uploading videos about remote-controlled airplanes to YouTube.

Here's the story behind his Click Millionaire business system. You'll see that it's one you could apply to almost any niche yourself.

Scott: Hi, Dave. People say you can make money in niches on the internet. But remote controlled airplanes, that's just a small niche for hobby nerds, right?

Dave: I know flying toys sounds pretty ridiculous. But I've been doing shows about remote-controlled "RC" airplanes on YouTube since 2006 or 2007. I fly airplanes and promote them on video. It's a lot of fun.

Scott: How did this get started?

Dave: My parents were looking for a hobby for me in high school, and my dad got me into remote-controlled airplanes. When I got older, I was working at a gym as a personal trainer. I was getting dissatisfied with the gym. I wanted to go somewhere in life, wanted to do something more. My buddy said, "You're a smart guy. Why don't you start your own business?" Mockingly I said, "Yeah and do what?" He replied, "I don't know. You like playing with remote-controlled airplanes on your lunch break. Do an RC airplanes business."

I jumped right into it, not knowing what I was doing, just a young entrepreneur, full of naiveté and energy. I started designing and selling RC airplane kits to guys on a popular online remote-controlled airplanes forum. I've never paid for advertising. I just went into the trenches on the forum, communicated with the members and slowly made friends to build up a little fan base; just super-serviced everybody when selling my kits. That went well but it got to be too much. I couldn't possibly keep up with manufacturing and building and shipping kits from a one-bedroom apartment.

Scott: So you started by making RC airplane kits and shipping them around the country?

Dave: Yes. Have you seen those photographs of people in Asia where they've got a bike, and then they've got these massive pallets and boxes stacked 10 feet high on the back? That's what I would do. I'd put these huge boxes on my bike, stack them higher than me and ride them down to the post office. That's what I did for a couple of years. My friends were embarrassed. But it got me a name in the world of RC hobbies and a customer base. It bought me some time as well to figure out how to start becoming a real entrepreneur, a real business guy, rather than an excited kid playing businessman on the Internet.

Scott: Then as you started to grow up you realized the Internet might make your work easier, and increase the profit margins too?

Dave: Yes, exactly. In my kit business I was selling the planes and parts. It started to get hard because a large company coming from China started selling directly to the consumers. That's what forced me to get silly and go, "How could I beat Goliath?" You can't go head to head. So I started to push my mind and ask questions. How can I win the hearts and minds of the RC community if I can't compete on price and product and all of that? Where is their weak spot?

My wife Val said, "We should do a YouTube account." This was the early days of YouTube, 2006, 2007. I'm like, "No, no. Don't do YouTube. I've seen that site. I don't have enough time, because I can't keep up with the little forums that I'm on right now. I don't want to deal with another forum."

Scott: You had been making some videos already to share in the forums?

Dave: Yeah, you're right. The videos were solving a problem. People would ask questions like, "How does the plane work? What do I need? How does this part go on?" I would tell them, "You know what, let me make a video and email it to all of you." But a lot of people said they couldn't play the videos on their computer. So for software simplicity, my wife set up a YouTube account anyway because she was tired of sending out media files. All of a sudden our model airplane videos got more views on YouTube in a week than a year and a half in the trenches on the forums. So I turned my attention to YouTube wondering how I could use it. I was very intimidated by it. I didn't know what to do.

Scott: How did you learn YouTube well enough to turn your channel into a star?

Dave: I thought about other things in my life that I had become successful at, but started out being intimidated and scared. I said, "How did I do that, how did I overcome it?" I realized it's familiarity, checking it out every day. It's like going to someone's house, you don't know your way around. If you go there 10 minutes every day, eventually you're going to find your way around.

The forum that I was good at was very intimidating when I first got into it. But going into it every day, it became my home. So I said, "Okay, Dave. Dedicate an hour or two every day going in and just playing around YouTube and get familiar with it." After a couple of months, I started to see the pattern of what the big players were all doing, even though their shows are very different. I started to understand the community from just being in there two hours a day. My friends and my parents would call and ask, "What are you doing?" I'd be like, "I've got to go. I've got to study YouTube." "Oh, come on. Look you have a great job at the gym. You leave that and sell toys on your bike, and now you're going to be a YouTube star?" I'm like, "Yeah, I'm going to be a YouTube star. I've got to go."

Scott: You're not a kid here, right?

Dave: I'm like 28 and married at the time, telling everybody I'm going to be a YouTube star. Their first question was, "What's YouTube?"

Scott: Okay, Dave. I know people are starting to wonder if you're for real. Can you share some metrics?

Dave: Sure, our average video now is 3–5 minutes long. It's anything from us experimenting with airplanes in a field or doing instructional videos for beginners. We have about 100 million views total so far. We get about 100,000 views a day on our YouTube channel that makes us several thousand dollars just from YouTube ads each month.

Scott: So YouTube alone is making you real money and your digital downloads business is even bigger than YouTube?

Dave: Yeah. We do the videos on YouTube and get paid for those. That's 100,000 views of free traffic each day that we can also direct wherever we want. We can steer all that to our website, or to another video. So the videos also promote our $47 ultimate course, which teaches people how to get started with RC airplanes. So we make our real money from selling the digital products that our videos promote. We sell those all day long through ClickBank. It's turning into real money, real quick.

Scott: A lot of people are intimidated by doing video. They think you need to have a big studio, and you need to do a lot of fancy production. But from the videos I've seen from you guys, it looks like it's just you guys and a hand-held camera out in the park flying an airplane. Did I miss the fancier ones?

Dave: We found that if your video stuff is too professional, people aren't going to watch it. People are going to the Internet because they are sick of TV. They are sick of overproduced, we-know-better-than-you presentations. The more real you are, the more people feel comfortable and connect with you. We played around with having a professional video guy make a couple of videos for us. We tested and gave it a good honest try. But then we looked at the numbers. We're like, "Wow this is going way the wrong way." Then we backed up towards dumbing down the production, keeping it more real. That's what connects with people on the Internet.

Scott: Let's talk about attracting an audience. You didn't buy any ads?

Dave: No, no. We tried some ads but when we looked at our numbers there, we just didn't like what we saw. With our particular business model it's better for us to take the time to produce videos to get our own traffic than to pay for ads. And one thing we found worked for us is to listen more to what the universe and the customers are asking for, not what we want to do.

Scott: What do you think the future looks like for people who are thinking about finding a niche of their own online? Is this over or are there still opportunities waiting?

Dave: The best is yet to come for people because they have people like you and I that have gone out and pioneered this and gotten our butts kicked. Anyone who is willing to listen to the experts and read books to get educated has such an advantage. That will greatly accelerate anyone.

Scott: In terms of your lifestyle, do you find making videos about remote-controlled airplanes a better career than your friends or relatives who are working office jobs?

Dave: Oh gosh, it really is. I live in Beaver, Oregon, a really nice place. We graduated from a one-bedroom apartment to a much larger house. I have the time to enjoy the bigger house and the neighborhood. And I've really got the work schedule down the way I like it. I'll work on RCs on the morning, go for a run, work on RCs in the evening, go for a bike ride or go to the coffee shop. Money doesn't solve all of your problems, but it sure solves a lot of them. And the energy that I have now is more than I've ever had in my entire life, just because my whole being just feels better, more balanced and energized.

Scott: Any last words to share with the folks?

Dave: Discover your passion, drive hard-core everyday and it builds up over time.

Visit Dave's YouTube channel at www.youtube.com/rcsuperpowers to see all his remote-controlled airplane videos in action.

How to Make Money Posting Video Clips Online

As you read this, people are out there using YouTube as a search engine to find answers to their problems, to learn things, and be entertained. Those are all opportunities for you as a Click Millionaire entrepreneur to publish videos that help them meet those needs. Whatever your niche is, there is an audience waiting to watch videos about it online. You can use YouTube as a channel to promote yourself, and then make money from the promotions themselves, too. That's what Dave is doing. He's not only posting videos on YouTube to make money from the YouTube Partner advertising program, but the same videos he's posting are also driving traffic back to his instructional digital products that teach people how to make remote control airplanes. So his commercials are making him money, spreading the brand, and driving more sales, too. That's a win-win Click Millionaire system!

It's not too late for you to do this either. Video capabilities keep increasing online, and it's constantly getting easier and cheaper to produce and distribute videos, too. At the same time, more of us every day are carrying smartphones in our pockets that allow video streaming, and consumers increasingly choose to watch amateur video instead of big budget Hollywood films and network TV. Short, helpful, more authentic videos like the ones you can produce yourself are winning against the big boys and creating new Click Millionaire business opportunities for you.

> **CLICK MILLIONAIRES SECRET: Clips vs. Show**
> Most business people who post videos on YouTube do so for marketing purposes. They shoot short clips that are essentially infomercials. That can be a successful online marketing tactic—but did you notice that Dave talks

about his videos as a "show"? Even though the clips are only 3–5 minutes long, Dave tries hard to make them entertaining. Shifting your mindset from making commercials to "producing a show" can help you make your videos more entertaining and attract more viewers and income.

Steps You Can Take Today Toward Video Stardom

While video production sounds intimidating, it's easier than ever before, and cheaper than you expect. HD video on your big flat screen TV is great for watching movies but that expensive, high-quality production is just not necessary to create entertaining promotional videos online today. Today almost any digital camera, and even most smartphones, will shoot video. You can also use a webcam attached to your PC to shoot yourself or you can record screencasts of your browser activity or PowerPoint presentations. Most cameras include video recording software tools that can help you save your video to your hard drive, too. You can edit the videos using similarly included software, try online editing services (search Google for the latest and greatest ones), or buy software like Final Cut to edit the videos yourself. And, if you don't want to learn video editing, you can head to project marketplaces like Elance, Guru, or even Craigslist to find qualified video editors willing to work inexpensively on a project basis to pretty up your videos.

> **CLICK MILLIONAIRES SECRET: Lighting**
> *As a regular producer of videos myself, I have found the hardest part is the lighting. If you try to shoot outdoors the lighting can change by the minute! (Look back at the older videos on my YouTube channel to see darker-than-they-should-be clips for a laugh.) I've learned the hard way that is why most TV shows shoot indoors on a set—because they can control the light.*
> *Solution: Inexpensive video lighting kits are available online.*
> *I recommend products from Cowboy Studios. They offer packages of basic lights, tripods, and light-diffusing umbrellas for less than $100 on*

Amazon.com. *For a small investment these kits can help you light up the kitchen, den, or garage where you shoot to help your videos look more professional.*

How to Start Your Own YouTube Channel

Anyone can join YouTube and use it as a promotional tool. It's free.

Some basic pointing and clicking will allow you to select a video file from your computer's hard drive to upload it to the YouTube website. YouTube starts most new accounts with a limit of 10 minutes per video. As you upload more videos and prove that you are not abusing their system, YouTube will extend the length of videos you can share there for free to 20 minutes or more. That doesn't sound very long if you are accustomed to TV or movies, but it's probably as long as you need since most online viewers prefer shorter clips anyway.

Within minutes of upload your video will be visible to YouTube users worldwide for free. YouTube also provides free sharing code that lets you copy and paste that new video onto your own websites and lets your viewers spread it around the Web, too. If you want to consolidate your videos into a custom-branded page on YouTube to create your own channel, that's free, too.

Why are all these valuable services free? Because YouTube (which is part of Google) makes its money selling ads on those pages and on top of and in front of your videos. (It's those ads that are making the money for the YouTube Partners Program, after all.) If you later want to upgrade to a video hosting service that is ad-free, you can pay to use video hosting services like Wistia, Viddler, Vzaar, Vimeo, or Brightcove. This is a good idea if you are producing sales videos where you don't want advertising distracting your prospects.

CLICK MILLIONAIRES SECRET: Too Shy for Video?

The most common objection to video marketing online is one many people won't admit: they don't like the way they look on camera. If this is holding you back from creating your own video series, try shooting "screencast" videos. Camtasia is the most popular screen capture software for PCs, and ScreenFlow works similarly for Macs. You can use these tools to record any activity on your screen, including presentations, web browsing, slide shows, or even other videos. Add to that your offscreen voice narrating the video to explain what viewers are seeing and you soon have a good video with no hair, wardrobe, lighting, or makeup worries!

Other YouTube Stars

Other inspiring niche YouTube video success stories include:

- MPGomatic (www.youtube.com/mpgomatic): Dan Grey turned his love for cars into a business as creator, host, and brains of a YouTube channel that makes him money reviewing new cars (and he gets to drive the newest ones free.)

- Maangchi (www.youtube.com/maangchi): In 2007 Emily Kim started posting Korean cooking clips from her kitchen in Canada. Her Korean cooking show on YouTube now attracts viewers (and ad revenues) worldwide.

- Elle and Blair Fowler (www.elleandblair.com): These young ladies attract hundreds of millions of views to their YouTube videos. The sisters started with videos of their shopping "hauls" but today include beauty tips and fashion advice, too.

- Salman Khan (www.khanacademy.org): He started making videos to tutor his young cousins in math. The videos were so popular on YouTube that he started an online video education company. His KhanAcademy.org is on its way to revolutionizing schools with backing from the Bill Gates Foundation. (Bill uses the videos to tutor his own kids!)

‣ Andrew Lock (www.helpmybusiness.com): Built on his success marketing everything from potatoes to magic tricks, Andrew's free weekly web-based TV show, "Help! My Business Sucks!", offers marketing insight, answers viewer questions, and helps you "get more done and have more fun."

‣ Ryan Higa (www.youtube.com/nigahiga): While still in high school, Ryan and his friend Sean started posting YouTube videos of themselves lip-synching to popular songs. After their YouTube channel had all its videos removed because they were using unlicensed songs, Ryan started over with music he composed himself. Today Nigahiga's comedic song videos have been viewed over 1 billion times on YouTube.

And, don't forget the Click Millionaires channel on YouTube, and hundreds of "how to," getting started, web design review, and motivational videos free at www.ClickMillionaires.tv.

ClickMillionaires.com Member Bonus: Hear the inspiring story behind BallisLife.com! Former pharmacy technician Matt Rodriguez turned his love of basketball into a Click Millionaire lifestyle business system. He travels the country hanging with top NBA players to shoot fun videos that attract over 2 million page views/month to his website. Big name advertisers like Nike, Footlocker, EA Sports, Adidas, and Gatorade are happy to sponsor, too. Listen to a free podcast interview with Matt that's available to ClickMillionaires.com members. Use the special URL www.ClickMillionairesReader.com when you join!

CHAPTER 12 NOTE

1. Nielsen, 6/16/11; blog.nielsen.com/nielsenwire/online_mobile/may-2011-top-u-s-online-destinations-for-video/

13

social networking communities for fun and profit

WHAT'S LEFT of traditional business after global Internet competition drives profit margins down to zero and anything that can be copied is spread around the Internet for free? Will you still have a business when the worldwide reach of the Internet lets competitors give away your previously profitable products for low prices or even for free just to gain new customers or market share?

I see two viable categories left as the best foundations on which to build a long-term business system today:

▸ Original, real-time news and entertainment experiences.

▸ Relationships.

Unfortunately in news and entertainment, competitors constantly invent new forms of online experiences and information delivery to threaten those businesses. (No one at CNN saw Twitter coming!)

That leaves us with relationships.

Communities: My Favorite Click Millionaire Business Model

So let's take a look at my favorite type of Click Millionaire lifestyle business system: *relationship-based online communities.* We're all hard-wired for interaction and companionship. This genetic fact offers you Click Millionaire lifestyle business opportunities in building new businesses online that connect people.

Going online to chat with like-minded people is no longer limited to social activity after-hours or on weekends. It's an increasingly popular method for business interactions, too, including taking breaks from work or for people who work alone to socialize during the day. If your website becomes a hub where people interact with their friends daily, they are happy to visit repeatedly and they get locked in to participating where their important relationships are based. Plus, competitors can't create free versions of those friendships to compete with you.

Connecting previously dispersed audiences into relationship-based online communities obviously has been huge for social networks like Facebook but thousands of smaller businesses have tapped this trend successfully, too. As the Click Millionaire owner of your own social network, discussion forum, electronic bulletin board, membership service, or community, you can become the host of a 24/7 online party that serves just the types of people you want to hang out with or sell to.

Almost any topic can be the foundation for a community of your own. Ideally you'll target a topic or niche audience that leverages several of the moneymaking Click Millionaire Lifestyle Business Design

Success Principles detailed in Chapter 5. If you do, you could end up with a success story as surprising as the following one.

Click Millionaire Business Profile: BackYardChickens.com

Raising chickens sounds like a hobby for rural families. But you may be as surprised as I was to learn that city dwellers and suburbanites worldwide raise chickens at home, too. This offbeat hobby underlies the appeal of BackYardChickens.com, the world's largest online community dedicated to the raising of your own backyard flock.

The site started when a kindergarten class project introduced some baby chicks to an unsuspecting home. Dad went online to share some simple chicken coop designs. The more information he added, the more fellow chicken lovers visited. The visitors started adding their own chicken coop designs and asking questions, too, lots of questions. Soon there were too many questions coming in for any individual to answer them all. That led to Rob Ludlow's

purchase of the website and creation of the BackYard Chickens Message Board in 2007. Over time the site has grown to become the #1 resource for information on raising chickens in any urban, suburban, or rural backyard. With over 100,000 registered members and millions of posts in its forum, this niche is a lot bigger than you probably would have guessed. And it's addictive. BackYardChickens.com attracts more than 11 million page views/month, about 100 new members daily, and more than 8,000 new forum posts every day (more than five new posts every minute, 24/7!). What has led to all this traffic? Of course it starts with enthusiasm for chickens. As Rob says, "Chickens are a multi-purpose pet! Chickens eat the bugs and weeds in your yard, generate fantastic fertilizer, and of course are a pet that makes you breakfast!"

The site capitalizes on the trend toward local farming and organic food but more fundamentally, its success is based on people helping people. Anyone interested in raising, breeding, or caring for their own chickens can find answers and new friends at BackYardChickens.com, any time day or night. The site is full of helpful articles and a forum filled with information about chicken coops, chicken breeds, feeding chickens, hatching chicken eggs, and chicken predators.

BackYardChickens.com makes money from its members primarily through advertising sales, both from Google AdSense and direct sponsorships from companies interested in reaching its chicken-raising audience. It also has a small online store offering books (Rob is coauthor of both *Raising Chickens for Dummies* and *Building Chicken Coops for Dummies*), temporary tattoos, bumper stickers and coffee mugs with the BackYardChickens.com logo, as well as "Golden Feather" memberships that offer upgraded storage and an enhanced profiles for members who want to support the otherwise free site for $20/year.

The site is so popular that it doesn't need to do much marketing. Owner Rob Ludlow says "The site grows through the slow and steady process of creating fantastic content and a wonderful user experience. People link to our site because it is the best in the niche and share it with their friends. The search engines also pick up on this and drive significant traffic for free."

Rob runs the business and technical operations himself, and over time has built a team of 15 of "the world's best moderators" to help manage day-to-day site operations. The fun parts of the business include quitting his day job in 2008, working from home, meeting and working with amazing people, and being featured in major media, including *USA Today*, the *Wall Street Journal*, *Entrepreneur Magazine*, and more. Rob says, "The flexibility to do what I want, when I want, doing what I love has been amazing!"

BackYardChickens.com is the lead example in this chapter because it demonstrates how *any* niche can be used to build a community-based business system online. Rob has found success even though the site is not fancy and modern looking. Instead he has successfully focused on serving the needs of his very specific niche and encouraged camaraderie among his audience members. This helpful and friendly approach is exactly what would cause you to join a community in the real world and it works online, too.

More Community Success Stories

Other examples of online community success include:

▸ *Architizer.com.* A community for architecture, Architizer.com is the only social network built exclusively for the people, projects, firms, and products of the global architecture industry. The free, advertising-supported site serves an important B2B function in the architecture industry by sharing news, jobs openings, and competitions that allow thousands of architects and related industry professionals a place to develop relationships and showcase their work. (www.architizer.com)

▸ *TuDiabetes.org.* After being diagnosed with type 1 diabetes, Manny Hernandez found that information from fellow diabetes sufferers was critical to managing the disease better and improving his daily life. He started his site for diabetes patients in 2007. It has since grown to attract more than 20,000 members who enjoy helping, educating, and socializing with each other in the site's busy forums, as well as helped Manny start the Diabetes Hands Foundation, a non-profit dedicated to diabetes education. The site's success also led to Manny authoring *Ning for Dummies*, which explains the best ways to use the popular social networking platform that he uses himself to power TuDiabetes.org. (www.tudiabetes.org)

▸ *VANetworking.com.* Tawnya Sutherland runs the largest community for virtual assistants online. With over 15,000 registered members, her free site helps virtual assistants learn how to service clients, find new jobs, take training classes, and develop the relationships needed to grow their business and support each other along the way. She makes money from advertising on this busy site as well as offering three different levels of membership upgrades. Her site's success has even been profiled on the *Dragon's Den* TV show in Canada. (www.vanetworking.com)

▸ *CommunityCare.co.uk.* A specialist website dedicated to all areas of the social care profession in the United Kingdom, this popular site and community grew out of *Community Care* magazine. It brings together social workers from across the United Kingdom for mutual support in its CareSpace forum. (www.communitycare.co.uk)

▸ *PbNation.com.* The #1 online community for paintball warriors, PbNation grew out of Tony Rieker's high school hobby. He started the bulletin board while on Christmas break and ran it with some friends until it got so popular that his dad, Ed, joined to turn it into a business. Today the site makes money from ads (mostly for paintball-related products) as well as from selling branded merchandise and offering membership upgrades. With hundreds of thousands of members and tens of millions of posts in its forum, PbNation is a great example of a niche interest that its owners have scaled into such a good Click Millionaire business that their PR rep says it was recently sold for $3.2 million. (www.PBnation.com)

› *CatholicMom.com.* Lisa Hendey shares her faith with moms worldwide through her website. Organized around blog posts and articles rather than a forum, her site's more than 100 contributing writers and columnists produce fresh content daily to keep readers returning and advertisers happy. (www.CatholicMom.com)

› *Gh0stMarket.net.* Yes, even criminals take advantage of online communities to build illicit businesses. Gh0stMarket.net was a UK-based forum run by teenagers that allegedly had more than 8,000 members trading credit card numbers, hacking tips, and even bomb-making info until it was busted in 2009.

My Own Community Success Stories

Communities are also my favorite online business model because I have made a lot of money building them myself. In fact, I have recruited my whole family into running profitable online communities!

I've been promoting the moneymaking potential of social networks, membership sites, and online communities since my first book, *Internet Riches.* I wrote that book after the success of BillOReilly.com, the membership community I helped Fox News commentator Bill O'Reilly build starting in 2002. A new website separate from the official *O'Reilly Factor* TV show website, at BillOReilly.com we went far beyond a then typical broadcaster's website to build a multimillion-dollar online community with tens of thousands of members worldwide. For years since then, Bill's broadcast reach and often controversial commentary have kept the forums hopping with new members (who pay $4.95/month each) and also helped sell truckloads of books, shirts, pens, and even doormats to *Factor* fans worldwide.

Since I retired to focus on my own ventures and writing books like this one, part of my success has been with other online communities I have started, including:

‣ *ArtFairInsiders.com.* This social network is dedicated to fine artists and the art fair industry. Now run by my own mother (a veteran of the art fair scene), thousands of artists visit the site daily to catch up on the latest art fair news, trade show tips, and swap gossip. The #1 community site in its niche and growing, it's free to members because advertisers who want to reach artists and art fair organizers love it. (www.ArtFairInsiders.com)

‣ *SweaterBabe.com Knitting Pattern Club.* My wife is a well-known knitting pattern designer. SweaterBabe.com features her stylish, modern knitting designs and is one of the most popular PDF knitting pattern download sites online. I also talked her into starting her own community online in 2009. Today hundreds of members pay $7.99/month for exclusive and early access to her latest knitting patterns. (www.SweaterBabeClub.com)

‣ *ClickMillionaires.com.* By now you know about my lifestyle business entrepreneurship coaching community. Our mission is to help new online entrepreneurs develop their own lifestyle businesses and learn online marketing, so as a reader of this book, it's free to you to join. It's known as one of the friendliest forums online and you don't even need to have a website to participate. (www.Click MillionairesReader.com)

I invite you to visit all of these examples to find successful business, community management, and marketing practices that you can use to build your own Click Millionaire community business system online, too.

The diversity of all these examples is meant to demonstrate to you that almost any niche interest can be used as the basis for an online community business today. Where there are interests, there are people. Where there are people, there are problems to be discussed, jokes to be traded, relationships to be built, and advice to be given. That's pretty much the definition of a community in the "real world" and now increasingly those e-communities are enabled online by inexpensive social networking platforms that you can adapt to your own lifestyle business purposes.

Success Factors for Online Communities

Online community businesses are good lifestyle businesses because they include almost all of the Click Millionaires Lifestyle Business Design Success Principles detailed in Chapter 5. Online communities can *help people*, can be *automated* and *outsourced*, position you as an *expert*, are *scalable*, offer *recurring revenue*, plus the audience creates much of the *content* for you. If you review the several online community examples included here, and maybe even join a few, you'll notice several additional community-specific success factors that they have in common. You can apply these factors to help develop your own online community. Successful online communities:

- Serve specific niche needs rather than general ones.

- Focus on helping their members.

- Encourage members to help each other, too.

- Are not too concerned about implementing the latest bells and whistles of technology.

- Don't spend much (if any) time or money on marketing because the audience recruits its friends for free.

The last factor that makes online communities my favorite Click Millionaire business opportunity for you is that they are downright cheap to operate and can be a lot of fun to run! If you pick a target market that interests you, then you can grow an online destination where you get to be the host, set the agenda, and collect the revenues, too. As BackYardChickens.com's Rob Ludlow says, "Running such a large community has allowed me to meet and work with some of the most amazing individuals. It has been a fantastic experience being able to leverage my entrepreneurial and online skills and combine them with a joy/hobby to create something that is amazingly successful."

> ### CLICK MILLIONAIRES SECRET: Where Nice Guys Can Finish First
>
> *Online communities are great lifestyle businesses for "nice people." In fact, niceness can finally be an advantage in the business world if you are running a membership site. Because you only interact online, even shy or introverted entrepreneurs can make friends in online forums to build businesses where little face-to-face contact is required and politeness, caring, and helpfulness are actually valued. Over time your personality comes through and nice guys (and gals) finally have a true advantage!*

How Online Communities Make You Money

The business model for online communities is usually based on advertising. Because the focus is on members and encouraging their interaction, communities tend to generate a lot of page views. Once you install advertising code (whether from AdSense, affiliate ads, or custom sponsorships), those page views can start turning into money without much more work from you. This audience-contributed content and scalability (Click Millionaires Success Principles #5 and #6 respectively) are a large part of the reason I recommend communities.

It's true that far more people read than comment or post in online forums, but don't underestimate the importance of these "lurkers." While it's said that only 1 percent of people post a lot, and the next 9 percent of members do most of the commenting, it's that remaining 90 percent that ensures your ads get clicked on, too.

> ### CLICK MILLIONAIRES SECRET: Charging Advertisers vs. Charging Members
>
> *The money in most communities does not come directly from the members. In some cases you can create enough premium content, exclusive activities, or desirable upgrades to convince members to buy things or even subscribe to generate recurring revenues. More often, however, the revenue from online communities comes from advertisers who are service providers who want to promote their services to your members. If you do a good job of creating a community where a defined group of people enjoy hanging out, you may even be able to charge both the members and the advertisers!*
>
> *Many communities also include online stores offering various upsells. This allows them to sell merchandise related to the community's interests, or just logo-branded items that help members express their loyalty. You can also charge for one-time upgrades like access to special content or participation in online events like webinars or conference calls. If your content and audience will support it, the top business model for a community site is recurring membership fees. This strategy brings you recurring revenue for content that is largely audience-contributed if you create a friendly, helpful environment that encourages such participation. This is what I do for the Premium Memberships levels of Click Millionaires (although basic access is free to you as a reader of this book!).*

The Best Ways to Build Your Own Community Online Today

Following Facebook's success, many companies offer tools to help even nontechnical entrepreneurs build their own social networks. I prefer hosted services because they are easier for nontechnical users to manage. Some of the better ones include:

Ning (www.ning.com)

SubHub (www.subhub.com)

SocialGo (www.socialgo.com)

MemberGate (www.membergate.com)

Wild Apricot (www.wildapricot.com)

There are also many programs ("scripts") available for purchase online that can be used to add forums, pay walls, and other members-only features to a website, as well as a variety of plug-ins and tools for WordPress that can be used to introduce and manage community features on WordPress sites.

How Much Does It Cost?

Today you can build your own customized Facebook-style social network website very inexpensively. The technology needed to start your community online ranges in cost from one-time licensing payments of between $20 and $300 for membership scripts you install on your own servers to monthly fee-based services of between $5 and $500/month for hosted services. Between $20 and $50/month will get you started with a high-quality hosted service. A budget that small can be recouped with just a few sales or paying memberships per month. As Connie Mettler of ArtFairInsiders.com says "I think that people would be amazed at how cheap it is to run an online community—all it takes is some time!"

You can build a great-looking social network of your own just by pointing and clicking, especially if you choose to use a browser-based service like Ning, shown in Figure 13–1. You don't have to know any technology, so you can concentrate on developing a good niche strategy and activities that will engage your audience and encourage them to recruit their friends, too.

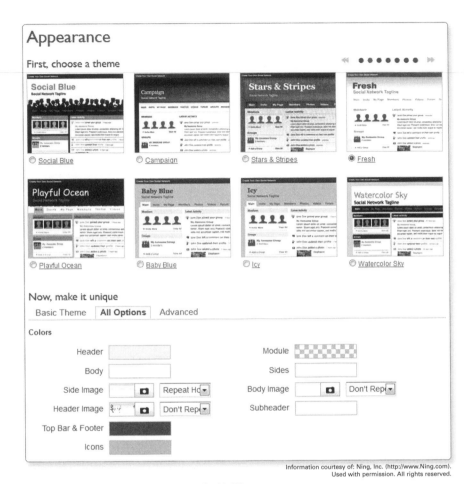

Figure 13–1. Choosing an "Appearance" with Ning.

CLICK MILLIONAIRES SECRET: Why Not Just Build My Community on Facebook?

With its huge worldwide audience and powerful, free social network tools, many Click Millionaires wonder why they shouldn't just use Facebook to start their online communities. Here are a few reasons:

▸ *You don't control the branding.*

▸ *You don't control the layout.*

▸ *You don't own your customer audience data.*

▸ *You don't control changes to the Terms of Service or Privacy Policy.*

▸ *You don't control the ads (or make money from them).*

*These issues don't matter much if you are just having fun online, but if you are running an online community **to make money** you need to control the site yourself. Use Facebook to promote your community to attract more members, but drive them over to your own site if you want to make money. Come join us at ClickMillionaires.com today to see how it's done!*

14

easy digital download and information product sales

"HOORAY, MOMMY!" That's what SweaterBabe.com owner Katherine hears every time she turns on her computer. Every sale from my wife's popular knitting pattern download website triggers another alert and the recorded voices of our kids call out to congratulate her. With hundreds of sales daily, the PC is sometimes noisier than our real children! Can you imagine setting up your email program to ring a bell, offer applause, or shout encouragement every time your website confirmed another transaction? It's a fun and easy way to reinforce your digital sales success (and it really impresses guests, too!)

Selling things to each other is one of the most traditional forms of interaction. The Internet has enabled a new kind of "virtual selling" that you can profit from, too. This is the sale of information products distributed as digital files.

Instead of opening a store to sell products to walk-in customers or even taking orders online for home delivery by UPS, a proven Click Millionaire business system is to sell downloadable digital files that are delivered instantly and automatically through the Internet. With just a few clicks your online customers can find, pay for, and transfer to their own PCs these digital products they buy from you.

A few examples of digital files you can sell as downloads include:

documents	videos
music	drawings
recipes	photographs
patterns	software programs
e-books	diagrams
instruction guides	

Anything that can be saved as a digital file on your hard drive can be uploaded to your website for e-commerce sale online. This Click Millionaire business system may seem obvious, but I wanted to tell you about it because it has one huge advantage that I often see new entrepreneurs overlook: Download sales can be *far more profitable* than the sale of physical products.

How to Make Money Selling e-Books and Info Products

By eliminating so many of the costs incurred by traditional store operations, digital-only online retailers have an immediate head start over their bricks-and-mortar competitors. And because the purchaser only downloads a copy of a digital file (not the original), a single digital file can be sold repeatedly with no inventory concerns and virtually no additional distribution costs! It might cost you $100/month to run the website, shopping cart, and marketing tools for your business, but those costs don't change if you sell a single download—or a thousand. If your product sells for $25, you only need to sell four each month to cover $100 of costs. And if you sell 1,000 files that month, your cost is still only $100, leaving you with $24,900, and a 99.6 percent profit margin!

For practical insights on digital download sales, I spoke to Beau Blackwell from leading information product marketplace, ClickBank.

CLICK MILLIONAIRE INTERVIEW:
Beau Blackwell, ClickBank Client Knowledge Guru

Scott: What types of files are most popular to sell online?

Beau: The ways that people create and deliver digital products have shifted over the years. E-books are a really common format today but other types of digital downloads are video files, audio files, or even a piece of software. An e-book isn't really anything except a digital copy of a document delivered in an Adobe PDF format. Some people deliver them in Microsoft Word format, too. You just create a how-to guide on organic gardening or training your dog to behave better. It's as easy as writing it up in Microsoft Word and then converting the format to a PDF, which can be read on all kinds of different devices. Then someone buys it from you, whether it's through ClickBank or through your own website or a different type of platform, and then you deliver the digital download to them.

Scott: So if you're selling digital downloads, you're creating content or information that you put into a file of one format or another. Then you put an e-commerce shopping cart in front of the product and customers pay you for access online. It sounds like the big distinction is that it's not physical. A "digital product" is not a pair of shoes or a bag of dog food or a bottle of shampoo or a car part. It's information you package into something that could be emailed or offered by download.

Beau: Yes, absolutely. I call it "information product marketing" because most of the time you're creating a product based on what you know or to satisfy a certain need or problem that people have. Then you deliver that knowledge packaged as a download-able solution.

Scott: Can you give some examples of products based on personal knowledge.

Beau: Yes. It's such a broad range of topics that the only limit is probably your imagination. In the ClickBank marketplace we have hundreds of different product categories, but I've seen everything from an e-book on how to attract more humming-birds if you're a gardener, to products on how to raise your kids, how to fix your car, and how to train for a marathon. The point is that everyone is an expert at something. Even if you don't think you are, you probably are and you just take it for granted because it's what you do every day. It could be related to your job as an accountant for nonprofits or your hobby of gardening or snowboarding or simply your life experience. You can almost certainly turn your knowledge into a product by thinking about what would people who are just getting into it want to know about the subject. Or by sharing how you dealt with challenges when you were first learning so that you can help other people get past them quickly.

Scott: So it sounds like you're serving needs by providing a lot of how-to advice in niche categories?

Beau: Yes. "How-to" definitely lends itself to this because of the way people find the products. Nowadays that often is by searching on Google or through social networks like Facebook. These aren't the types of products that people would go and look up in the Yellow Pages. They are products that crop up when the customer is researching online trying to solve a problem. Somebody can be online in the middle of the night or looking for an answer for something on the weekend. They find your product online, buy it, and get immediate access. Download sales let you solve people's problems right then rather than them having to visit stores or go see an expert to get their question answered.

Scott: You're suggesting that a lot of the success for information products is selling things that people wouldn't know where to go to find. They can't go over to Target or Walmart and buy it. There's isn't a book easily available for someone interested in breeding Australian parakeets or something obscure.

Beau: You're right to focus on that niche point because a lot of people think, "Oh, I've got to find a massive market with a lot of potential customers to make a lot of money." But the great thing about the digital and information product model is that you don't necessarily need all that many people buying from you all the time because your overhead is really low. If you can get even a small market, you can make a nice income off of that. The other cool thing is that you can get customers from around the world. So unlike if you're going to set up a brick and mortar shop, you can have people buying from you in Australia in the middle of the night. Typically new orders get fulfilled immediately online without you having to do much manually.

Scott: What are the lifestyle benefits of the information products approach that a new entrepreneur would want to factor into their start-up equation?

Beau: The number-one benefit is the freedom. It's such a key thing today where the job world is pretty uncertain and even if you feel secure, you may not be. You can avoid being told where you have to be and when you have to be there every single day. You are able to take time off and do the things you want to do, or go out in the middle of the day when it's a nice day like it is today here in Colorado. The entrepreneurs I know that are in the information product space are not only working 10 minutes a day and getting rich. Some of them work really hard but they just get to work on their own terms. They work from a coffee shop or they work from 10:00 p.m. to 2:00 a.m. and then sleep in the next day. It's really just being able to make your own choices, design your own lifestyle, and not have to work for The Man. Online you can access your customers 24 hours a day so you don't have to physically be anywhere for your business to be able to happen and that's really cool.

Scott: How much does it cost to get started? Don't all the traditional costs of office space and insurance and electricity and parking and furniture and advertising and all that fade away when you do information marketing?

Beau: Yes. It is amazingly inexpensive to get started, especially now. Even just five years ago, it could be kind of expensive to get a website designed and purchase some of the technology platforms. Today, it's almost silly how inexpensive it is. You probably can get started for under $100 to have a website, web hosting, a domain name, have your product up and available for sale, and actually be able to take and fulfill orders. You could probably get to that point within a week or so.

You also get to decide how to grow your business. I know a lot of people who are still a one-man or one-woman show that are doing six figures in sales a year and don't have or want any employees. I know other people who just hire virtual assistants for four hours a week or for however much time they need help. So really it's kind of up to you to scale the costs and business to fit the lifestyle that you want to live.

Scott: Great point. There's that word again, lifestyle.

Beau: Yes. I know guys who have told me, "I could easily be doing double in sales what I am right now, but I would have to work an extra 10 hours a week and I don't really want to do that." Others have said things like, "I want to go and live in the south of France for half the year, so I've built the business to support that lifestyle." I love hearing those stories. It's so great to be able to make those choices and live the way you want to.

Scott: What are typical price points for digital products selling on ClickBank?

Beau: It varies pretty widely. Our average product is somewhere in the $30 to $40 range. That might sound high for an e-book, but that's another one of the cool things about information products as compared to traditional books or CDs or DVDs. A lot of people getting into the information product industry think, "I couldn't sell my e-book for any more than traditional books or traditional DVDs. Why wouldn't someone just buy a regular book?" But that's just not the case. As long as the product solves their problem or teaches them what they need to know, you would be amazed at how much people are willing to spend to get exactly what they're looking for.

An e-book may only be 100 pages long, but you can charge $40 or $50 for it and the customers are absolutely happy as long as it speaks to their needs.

I'll use dog training as an example. A person has gotten a new puppy and the puppy has been chewing up everything, peeing in the house, and digging up the yard for the past week. They're about to lose their minds so they go online. They search for, "How do I get my Australian shepherd to stop chewing on things." They find an e-book on your website that says "I'll teach you exactly how to get your Australian shepherd to stop chewing in the next hour." Do you think that person, at midnight on a Saturday night, is going to be willing to spend $10 extra to get their dog to quit chewing up everything in their house? Absolutely. They don't want to wait until the next day. They just want to get their problems solved right then, so they're more than happy to spend that extra money.

Scott: And that translates into more money for you because your costs are pretty minimal. You've got a website and a one-time $50 listing fee if you list your product for sale through ClickBank. After that, download sales are pretty much profit because you've already written the book and it's a sunk cost. If you sell one of those or you sell a thousand, it doesn't cost you any more after that. Of course, marketing is a big variable there, but if you can do some marketing and attract some sales, the profit margins are pretty high.

Now I know my readers like numbers. What metrics can you share about ClickBank?

Beau: We've been around for about 13 years now and our sales have grown steadily every year. As far as payouts, we've paid out more than $2 billion to our affiliates and vendors. We have 15,000 to 20,000 product vendors who create, sell, and deliver information products, software, or any kind of digital goods like that. We have about 50,000 actual products that are for sale in our marketplace right now.

One more thing about ClickBank is that we also have over 100,000 affiliates who may be interested in marketing on your behalf in exchange for a commission. So those are 100,000 semi-professional Internet marketers who look regularly at ClickBank and say, "Is there something here I could promote to my audience?" and if they pick out your stuff they sell it for you. You have to pay those affiliates but only if they make a sale so it's a pretty good win-win situation.

Scott: Do you think there is still opportunity for new information product entrepreneurs?

Beau: Oh, there are definitely opportunities. I'll give you a specific example. One of our top product creators and sellers makes over a million dollars a year and he just got started two years ago. Before that he had never sold anything online and he and his partner went into the super-competitive health and fitness niche. There are thousands of products already in that niche, but they went literally from zero to seven figures in two years just by really focusing, doing a good job of making sure that their product met people's needs, treating their affiliates well, and always working to improve their sales process.

So it's absolutely not too late. People always have issues that they need help with and it's getting easier and easier to reach them online. With e-commerce technology being cheaper and easier to use than it ever has been this is really the best time ever to get started.

Wow! $2 billion in payouts to digital download sellers! And, of course, CickBank is not the only place to sell information products online. Keep in mind that the longer you wait, the more competitive things get but it's far from too late. As Beau suggested, it's always a good time to start.

Success Factors for Digital Information Products

Let's review some of the success factors that Beau pointed out:

1. *Serve needs and solve problems:* Serve a need outside of your own need to make money by helping people solve problems in their lives. Niche information products can help customers who are looking for niche solutions, and digital file sales are a great way to deliver them. Build your products around those solutions and you're going to have a lot better sales. That little trick or technique you worked out to make your own life better, the obstacles you've overcome, or that problem you helped your family fix, can all be turned into money. Those sorts of solutions are what other people are seeking. And with the connectivity of the web, Google can reach all those wannabe problem solvers and direct them to your product.

2. *Big returns for low costs:* You can literally write up a document in Microsoft Word to create your product. Then you can sell the same digital file over and over and over again. Your inventory is unlimited and your profit margins are very high. This is a great example of Click Millionaires Success Principle #3: Automation and Success Principle #6: Scalability. And if you use ClickBank's affiliate marketing network to promote the products, you can include Click Millionaires Success Principle #4: Outsourcing in there as well.

3. *Instant gratification:* Digital delivery also takes advantage of what I call the "Convenience Principle." People want information and products when they want them and how they want them. People love immediate delivery and offering it can make you money from impulse purchases online. If you can satisfy this Convenience Principle, the price matters less. A specific answer to my specific problem that I can get right now? That sells well at almost any price.

How to Get Started Selling Downloadable Files

Create a file of whatever your audience will find valuable. It could be your commentary on the latest political issues, blueprints for building new homes, MP3s or videos of your band, just about anything. Then upload the files to your website or store. To sell your digital files you'll likely want to use an established e-commerce platform. Most full-featured e-commerce shopping carts today can allow you to sell downloads alongside any physical goods you may already be offering online. For example I use one from my own Internet MillionaireDomains.com that costs just $8.99/month. You can also use services that specialize only in download file sales like e-Junkie, Payloadz, or ClickBank.

> **CLICK MILLIONAIRES SECRET: The Fastest, Cheapest Way to Sell Online**
>
> The simplest way to sell downloads is to join PayPal as a merchant. When you do you'll have access to their free "buy button" tools. With a few clicks and some quick copy and paste, you can install "Buy Now" buttons on your Web pages that will let your customers send you money for purchases. Upload your digital product file to a page on your website and set your PayPal checkout button to automatically deliver new purchasers to that page after they make payment. You can post the link to the file there for new customers to download it right away. When someone pays you for a digital file, PayPal sends you their money and delivers them automatically to the download page. You'll get an email confirmation for each order detailing the money received, too. Congratulations, Click Millionaire!

PART FOUR

IF YOU DON'T HAVE

A PRODUCT OF YOUR OWN

· · · · · · · 15 · · · · · · ·

marketing and promoting other people's products

IF YOU DON'T have a product of your own or don't want to invest in creating one, you can use email, social media, podcasting, blogs, online video, and all the tools we have discussed in earlier chapters to make money from other people's products. When promoting other people's products, you start with an already proven product and use your own skills to make money by discussing, reviewing, or promoting it online. This is a good strategy if you like to promote things, if you enjoy "sharing" in social media like Pinterest, Twitter, or Google+, if you like to shoot YouTube videos, if you have an interest in interviewing people or reviewing products, and if you would like to avoid much of the writing, research, and production usually required to create new products.

Online Promotions Services

You can start an online business like these, which offer promotional services to businesses that want to reach your target market:

‣ At AnyLuckyDay.com advertisers pay founder Giancarlo Massaro to promote and give away a new product each day. He also promotes the sponsor's product by creating a YouTube video about it, tweeting about it, posting on Facebook, and emailing his subscriber list. The audience  gets a chance to win each day's prize by simply leaving a comment on his site and the sponsor gets great online and social media exposure.

‣ Jason Sadler helps companies reach new customers by wearing a different company t-shirt every day to promote each sponsor's product. As a human billboard he then shoots an original promotional video for YouTube, webcasts a live video show on Ustream, and shares photos across Facebook and Twitter, too. Jason has grown from being a solo operator in 2009 to employing four professional daily shirt-wearers across the United States for IWearYourShirt.com.

Many companies want to expand their brands online but are understaffed or still new to social media. Services like these make money by helping them spread the word online.

Reviews

You can also pick a niche and review the latest products and services other companies are selling to that niche. For example:

▸ Rumi Neely started her style blog "Fashion Toast" in 2008. Photos of her wearing different fashionable outfits with commentary were enough to attract the attention of fashionistas worldwide. Today ad sales (and lots of free clothes) help Rumi model, blog, and travel worldwide (for more modeling and blogging) to share the latest fashions with her audience.

▸ RottenTomatoes.com is a top movie reviews site but Senh Duong started it simply because he wanted to collect all the reviews of Jackie Chan movies he could find online into one place. Today it boasts more than 20 million visitors monthly and Warner Brothers owns the site.

▸ Ray William Johnson has the #1 most-subscribed-to channel on YouTube. He's attracted almost 2 billion views of his videos. What are his videos about? Reviews, criticism, and jokes about other viral videos!

Interviews

Simply asking questions can also be the foundation of a Click Millionaire business.

▸ Wayne Hurlbert interviews the authors of new business books on his Blog Business Success Radio podcast show and reviews the books on his Blog Business World blog, too. As one of Blog Talk Radio's most enduring podcasters he has interviewed more than 400 leading business book authors, CEOs, business visionaries, and entrepreneurs since he started in 2006. In addition to enjoying working from his home in Winnipeg, Canada, Wayne's interviews and reviews attract business to his SEO and social media consulting business, too.

▸ Andrew Warner has a similar interview-based business called Mixergy. His interviews are usually video chats with start-up company founders. He has interviewed hundreds of entrepreneurs and also compiled what he has learned from those conversations into dozens of online courses. His audience loves his "business tips for successful start-ups" approach and Andrew makes money through a combination of sponsorships, course fees, and premium membership sales.

Affiliate Marketing

Another way to become a Click Millionaire is by participating in affiliate programs. This type of online marketing can make you money for each sale that you deliver to a merchant from ads you place on your site or in your emails. Sales commissions can range from a small percentage to hundreds of dollars from each sale.

While affiliate marketing is often promoted as a business in and of itself, I see it more as an ad strategy for making money after you have already collected an audience. Like multilevel marketing (which we'll discuss in the next chapter), it can be challenging to make money if you don't yet have an audience or if you only represent one product as your entire business. But, if you have developed an audience and then you join the affiliate programs of merchant companies that sell quality goods or services which are a good match to your audience's interests, affiliate marketing can be easy, inexpensive, and very profitable.

See Chapter 24, The Secrets of Online Advertising, for details on my favorite affiliate programs and how marketing other peoples' products online can be a low-risk Click Millionaire lifestyle business strategy.

Flash Sales and Daily Deals

There is also room for more "deals" sites targeted to niche audiences. While Woot.com does a great job of offering daily deals on technology products, and Haute Look and Gilt.com cover clothing and high-end fashion well, there are thousands of other niches where targeted audiences could be developed to help you make money promoting or reselling third-party products. How about daily deals for plumbers or contractors who are always buying more materials? Or travel bargains for families, medical supply deals for senior citizens, restaurant furniture and supplies deals for restaurant managers, boating equipment sales for yacht owners, or discounts on dental tools for dentists?

▸ ▸ ▸

You could apply the strategies above to almost any topic. There are few niches that aren't ready for more targeted social media promotions, videos, giveaways, affiliate offers, reviews, VIP interviews, or deals. The companies in each niche need publicity for their new products (and are often willing to pay for it), while the audience wants to hear about them, too. Put yourself in the middle of that equation in a field that you enjoy and you are on your way to a profitable Click Millionaire lifestyle business system.

Drop Shipping Is Not the Answer

A ClickMillionaires.com member from the United Kingdom wrote recently to ask:

> Dear Scott,
>
> I'd like to know what the pros and cons are of drop shipping, and how you go about starting.
>
> Thanks,
> Liz
> Cumbria, UK

Here's how I answered Liz:

> Hi Liz,
>
> It sounds like you may have been charmed by the promise of drop shipping, many entrepreneurs new

to online business are. But it's not the instant online moneymaking solution you're hoping for.

It's true that drop shipping can allow you to sell quality products without having to invest in inventory. It's a lot easier to forward customer purchase orders directly to a manufacturer or distributor for shipping than to fulfill them yourself, too. But researching drop shipping is the wrong first step when starting a new business because it suggests that you should pick out products to sell <u>before</u> you have identified a passion, found a target market with needs you can fulfill, developed a differentiating online marketing plan, etc. The lists of drop shipping suppliers you see promoted online may be helpful, but it's just as likely that your e-commerce business will sell ads, info products, or affiliate products.

My advice? Save (or at least postpone) the money you're going to spend on a drop shipping service "membership." Start instead by developing a personalized e-business strategy that serves customer needs and build an audience around that. Then go look for products that serve those needs.

Best,
Scott Fox

Note: I'm not a drop shipping expert myself so I tried to answer this question in more depth when researching this book. I contacted the CEO of a top drop shipping information firm to be interviewed on my Click Millionaires Success Show podcast. He was friendly at first but then canceled our interview after researching me! Needless to say, I remain skeptical . . .

·　·　·　·　·　· 16 ·　·　·　·　·　·

network marketing
the truth about mlm

I'VE ALWAYS BEEN skeptical about multilevel marketing (MLM). Selling overpriced products to friends and family sounds more likely to lead to uncomfortable situations than easy money. But I've been hearing that MLM has found new life online so I dug into network marketing as part of the research for this book. Here's an eye-opening new take on MLM that I hope is helpful to you.

If you've spent any time researching business opportunities, you've likely come across network marketing (also known as multilevel marketing or direct selling) more than once. The MLM industry is good at attracting aspiring sellers with promises of easy earnings and exciting prizes for top sellers. Selling MLM products sounds easy because as a new recruit, you are trained to sell detergents, cosmetics, vitamins, services, or whatever to your personal network of friends, family, and acquaintances. Then as you start selling the products to your personal networks, hopefully you recruit some of those friends to become subdistributors, too. As the people "beneath" you in this sales hierarchy start selling, you receive a portion of each their sales as commission.

This is the appeal of network marketing: You can quickly become a "manager" by building your own organization of salespeople. If you do that, you can stop selling products yourself and collect a cut of each sale that your team makes instead. This chain of distributor relationships creates multiple levels of compensation based on each salesperson's place in the hierarchy of what is called the "downline" of the product's sales organization. This ability to get paid both for sales you make yourself and to also participate in the sales made by people you recruit is why it's called "multilevel" marketing. And because you recruited the salespeople from your own network it's also commonly called "network" marketing, too.

Now, the results of my research. I found good news and bad news to share with you.

First, *the good news:*

If you have never worked for yourself before, network marketing can be a friendly introduction to entrepreneurship. The better network marketing companies provide their new recruits with training, professionally produced materials, even camaraderie and fun as part of larger team.

There's good money to be made in network marketing, especially if the company you join allows you to leverage modern online marketing techniques. The Internet has breathed new life into the recruiting of friends, family, and acquaintances into your personal downline of sales representatives that can help make you money as a MLM product distributor.

The bad news is pretty much the same thing:

The Internet has made it so easy for people to find each other and share product information that traditional MLM recruiting and customer-acquisition techniques are not as effective anymore. Many MLM companies are under pressure because the Internet allows all of their distributors online at the same time. This competition makes it harder for you to differentiate your products as an MLM representative than it used to be. If your friends and cousins are promoting the same things to similar audiences, at the same prices, with the same delivery methods, then it's going to be hard for you to make money the same way.

To help figure out today's network marketing opportunities, I interviewed Ann Sieg. She's had success in traditional MLM businesses but also understands enough about online businesses to compare and contrast them. After all, if MLM does offer good opportunities today to build profitable lifestyle businesses, I am interested, too!

CLICK MILLIONAIRE INTERVIEW:
Ann Sieg, Network Marketing (MLM) Expert

Scott: What qualifies you as an expert on MLM?

Ann: I've been in network marketing for 24 years. I started when I was pregnant with my second child. In 2002 I went full-time. We lost our windshield repair business that we had owned for 12 years after legislation killed that industry. My husband ended up doing a bunch of odd jobs while I was busy working my network marketing business. Once I implemented my own attraction marketing methodologies, I grew an organization very rapidly. I basically went from $2,000 to $90,000 in 3 months in the summer of 2006.

I was able to bring my husband home to work with me and my son, who is my business partner.

We've gone on to make over 10 million dollars in online sales, 4 million dollars on just one of my books, and millions of dollars in other promotions. The smartest thing I ever did was to ignore the advice of my up-line and take my educational process into my own hands, because at the end of the day no one cares about your business more than yourself.

Scott: What problems do you see with network marketing today?

Ann: I find the term "network marketing" to be a bit misleading. Most MLM companies are extremely limited in what they teach you about marketing. A lot of folks end up failing because they're taught marketing methods that they don't feel good about using. I went online to look for different solutions outside the network marketing industry and thank heavens I did. That's when I began to learn the true essence of marketing.

Scott: How do you pick a company or a product and evaluate who the good ones are to work with?

Ann: There is no hard and fast answer but I would say there are certain things I look for. Does the company have a good grasp of marketing? What marketing model are they teaching and how tolerant are they of people implementing their own marketing practices?

You have to develop a marketer mindset to determine if there is a hungry audience for the products, or if there is market saturation. Finding a hungry, targeted audience with money is what marketing is all about.

Scott: That sounds like a real dose of cold water on all the MLM hype I've heard over the years. Are there still opportunities?

Ann: Yes. I have to tell you, the potential is so enormous. I do business all over the world. I've got business partners in Thailand, Singapore, and Argentina. We have the global economy literally at our fingertips. So it's really an amazing time to live in, but you have to learn marketing skills in order to reach out and participate in this global economy, so that you're in the driver's seat.

Scott: So marketing yourself is now a life skill?

Ann: That's exactly right! In this economy where jobs are down, I think the top order of the day is to develop your own skills and learn how to market yourself, because products do not get up and sell themselves. You've got to go out and market them.

Scott: So you would you recommend establishing diverse streams of income rather than focusing only on promoting one company's products?

Ann: Absolutely. If all you're doing is traditional MLM, that is really a faulty business model. I don't think it's a safe business model either. I know some people are like, "Why can't I just do one thing?" Well you can if you want, but it's unrealistic to think you can plan on building a residual income for life from just one company.

You want to be set up so that you have your own assets, content that you've created, marketing pieces, books, videos, and whatever to build a list. Your own list that can become a million-dollar list like mine has. Now you own a real business, because real business is when you're in the driver's seat. That's very empowering. My advice is to first learn marketing and how to build income on demand and then you can go out and market anything that you so choose.

Network Marketing Meets the Internet—Ah Ha!

Network marketing always seemed like more enthusiasm than substance to me, as if there was supposed to be some sort of magic about it. But Ann's approach makes more sense: even in MLM, the bottom line is that *business is still business*. A lot of that other stuff is just hype and bad marketing training. You're not going to build a sustainable business by grabbing your kids' classmates parents, trying to recruit your cousins, or (as Ann says) "chasing down people in the shopping mall" to get random passersby to sign up for monthly deliveries of detergent, health drinks, vitamin supplements, or chocolate.

You shouldn't choose a company to represent simply because it claims that it has a great sales commission structure, or that its top producers will help you earn Mercedes or trips to Hawaii, or that their product has revolutionary health benefits. Like any other business venture, you should only invest your time in MLM opportunities that:

▸ Offer a good product that is differentiated from the competition.

▸ Allow you to market creatively online as much as possible.

▸ Appeal to an affluent, interested audience.

If you find an MLM opportunity that satisfies all three criteria, it's much more likely to be a real business, not just multilevel marketing hype. Now I'm more interested in multilevel marketing than I was before.

Notice that Ann's approach is Internet-based and she recommends that you create a business not just around a single product, but around yourself. That way MLM is just one of your income streams. That sounds a lot like a Click Millionaire system to me!

Questions to Evaluate Network Marketing (MLM) Opportunities

Next time you are approached about a multilevel marketing offer, why not look at it just like any other business opportunity? Before you get excited about the commission structure or the iPad you could win in the quarterly sales contest, look past the MLM peer pressure to ask yourself these questions:

- Is there demand for this product at this price?

- What marketing training does this company offer me?

- What restrictions are there on my marketing of the product?

- Can I set up my own website to promote it or do I have to use a company-provided website? (And, if so, what does that cost?)

- Is the market already full of similar products or other marketers?

- How can I differentiate myself and develop a cost-effective marketing plan to attract customers outside my friends and family?

- If I invest my time, reputation, and energy in promoting this company's products, what will I have built for myself as an asset if this company goes away unexpectedly?

- How will selling this product help me build an audience of my own or complement the other products I'm already selling to help me build a Click Millionaire business system with multiple income streams?

Like so many other industries, multilevel marketing has become Internet marketing. To be a successful network marketer today means you need to promote products that provide real value using cost-effective online marketing tools, not just beg your family members to buy more cosmetics or prepaid services.

So, while MLM can be a successful lifestyle business approach for a Click Millionaire, it is more of a strategy for monetizing an audience or niche interest than a business of its own. To figure out how you can best profit from it, go back to Part One of this book to figure out your lifestyle goals, and how you can build an audience that is happy to hear from you regularly. Once you do that, you can sell that audience MLM products (or anything else you would like) to create your own Click Millionaire lifestyle business success story.

Note: I'm pretty new to MLM but was pleasantly surprised to learn that it's not that different from "real" business after all. But, if you have experience in network marketing and would like to correct my impressions here or share your own experience with fellow entrepreneurs interested in network marketing, please visit the MLM section of the ClickMillionaires.com Forum to tell me what I missed and share your experiences to help others, too.

17

fun, flexible freelancing as a lifestyle design strategy

Title: *Full-time Freelance Artist*

Background: *Freelancing full-time since 2008, I have completed over 350 jobs. I began learning to draw, paint, and design at age two and it has been my passion ever since. I'm living my dream, and as my parents always told me, when you love what you do it hardly feels like work!*

Fast Fact: *I worked in the advertising industry for over a decade, but turned full-time freelancer in order to have a flexible schedule to care for and enjoy my family. With the vast resources and global* *community online, I'm able to make a living, doing what I love, while still having a life! What could be better than that?*

You Don't Have to Be a CEO

Most of this book is focused on starting a new business where you are the CEO. But there are other ways to find Click Millionaire success online. One of the easiest to start and most flexible to pursue is freelancing as an independent contractor.

As a freelancer you work on a project basis rather than going to the same office every day, reporting to the same boss, doing the same commute, having lunch with the same people, and all that sort of routine stuff. By working for others you can also avoid much of the hassle, responsibility, and administrative requirements of starting a formal business. Freelancing is still trading your hours for dollars but much more on your own terms and schedule than if you work a "real job."

The flexibility available to freelance contractors can help you reinvent yourself and create a great lifestyle by setting up a new practice or service-based business where you make money by serving the needs of other companies.

You'll get to:

› Work remotely.

› Pick the projects that you like.

› Set the price that makes each job exciting for you.

› Take time off to travel between projects.

› Dodge the stuff you don't like to do.

› Arrange your schedule around your own lifestyle priorities.

› Make extra money outside your current job on a part-time basis.

‣ Explore different career paths.

‣ Learn new skills.

That's the beauty of freelancing. You get to do what you want to do. While the pay is not always high, and freelance gigs don't provide health benefits, you can pick and choose to focus on projects that best meet *your* needs.

By accepting project work on topics that interest you or that require you to use new skills, you are getting paid to train yourself. As you continue, you can focus your expertise on those niches of projects you enjoy, command higher rates, and learn the business strategies your employers use to grow their own businesses so you can apply them when you launch your own Click Millionaire business, too.

How to Find Work as a Freelancer

You might say "That all sounds great but how do I find projects from clients willing to pay me?" Our good friend the Internet is back to help you once again. The newspaper "Help Wanted" ads have been replaced by online "project marketplaces." Just like eBay matches buyers and sellers of old stuff from your garage, project marketplaces help employers find independent contractors. These marketplaces host thousands of project requests for all sorts of freelance services that you can consider offering yourself.

Popular project marketplaces include: oDesk (www.odesk.com), Freelancer (www.freelancer.com), vWorker (www.vworker.com), Elance.com (www.elance.com), Guru.com (www.guru .com), and Hire My Mom (www.hiremymom.com).

These marketplaces help match companies that need outsourced services with independent contractors. In this case, the independent contractor can be *you*.

Do You Have the Skills?

You may never have thought you had the technical credentials needed to become a freelance contractor online. While it's true that many of the projects posted are information-technology related, trends in our society and business are pushing companies to use more project-based contractors for all kinds of services. On Elance.com alone right now there are 142,723 projects posted from 160,756 active clients who are looking for help with all sort of projects. The jobs that you will find posted today are not just for PHP programmers and Web designers, there are also projects posted looking for freelance salespeople, writers, video producers, even lawyers, engineers, and translators. If you don't have these more specialized skills, you can bid for assignments that only require basic computer skills and good common sense, like being an administrative assistant, or doing customer service. I even saw a project posted asking for help in checking grammar.

To confirm the potential of freelance employment as a Click Millionaire lifestyle business-building opportunity, I interviewed Fabio Rosati, the CEO of Elance.com.

CLICK MILLIONAIRE INTERVIEW:
Fabio Rosati, CEO of Elance.com

Scott: What kind of skills are the most popular on Elance and where might a person get started?

Fabio: The skills in demand are always evolving. So one of the key strategies is to understand what you're good at, but also understand what's in demand in the marketplace today. The ideal freelancer packages his or her skill set in a way that attracts the employer looking for that particular skill set.

For example, you may be a good graphic designer, but if you were able to position yourself as a graphic designer with experience in creating infographics, and maybe upload a couple of interesting examples to your portfolio, that will help you stand out and give you an edge in the market because there are a lot of people searching for infographics designers today.

Similarly with software development, if you take the time to study the software development kit for the Android mobile operating system, you can begin by winning small Android projects. Within a few months you will have a portfolio and some credentials in the community of Android developers and you'll win more work, because demand for Android coding experts is growing at over 800 percent year over year on our site.

Scott: Are there projects for people who are not so technical?

Fabio: Absolutely. For example, we have a large and a growing population of specialists in customer support. No small business is able to provide 24/7 answering of phones or email follow-up because hiring someone to do it full-time can be hugely expensive. So what small businesses do is find people who are willing to do remote customer support for them part-time in different time zones. They are able to have somebody always answering the phones, giving them coverage that they otherwise wouldn't be able to provide. The barriers to entry there are pretty low because the basic skills for customer service are just that you've got to be a polite, smart, and articulate person who can answer emails and phones.

Scott: What does it cost to find work using your service?

Fabio: It's free to hire and it's free to apply for job. There's a graphic designer in Los Angeles, Steve Soto, who started moonlighting as a graphic designer on Elance. He would only work on Elance in the evening and on weekends while he had a full-time day job. Fast forward two years later, he has his own company, he has his own employees, and is using Elance as the source of almost 100 percent of his new business. He needs premium marketing features to keep attracting clients, so also he pays for a membership in addition to taking advantage of all the free things that we offer.

Scott: Can you give an idea of the size of your market place?

Fabio: We have paid out close to $500,000,000 to freelancers through our platform; $160,000,000 of that has been in the last 12 months alone. That number is growing at close to 70 percent year over year right now and it's accelerating because the market for freelancers is expanding. More and more people are discovering the efficiencies of contracting online, and more and more people are comfortable with remote work and telecommuting. More businesses are coming to hire and posting more jobs, more talent is discovering the model and participating, so it's like a virtuous circle.

Scott: How much can people make?

Fabio: That depends on how much time you are going to put into it. Are you going to try to work 10 hours a day or 10 hours a week? We have people on Elance who are making between $40,000 and $50,000 a year and then we have people who are making hundreds of thousands of dollars. It all depends on how focused they are on the business.

Scott: How can freelance contractors be sure that they're going to get paid?

Fabio: That's one of the advantages of using of our platform. First we provide a lot of statistics about both sides. You can see how long a person has been active on our system. Who else have they worked with, how much money have they spent on freelance projects? How many jobs have they posted? We'll even show you things like the feedback that they have left about other freelancers they have employed, so that you can decide if they are fair and reasonable to work for. But in addition to that, when you decide to work through Elance you have two payment options.

Option A, if you want to work on a fixed-price basis, you can ask your client to put the money for your project in escrow. When you submit your deliverable we release the money to you. Option B is if you work on an hourly basis, our system automatically tracks your time and submits your timesheet to the employer. Then we collect the money and we guarantee that you'll get paid within five days.

Scott: What does it take to get yourself up and running on the site as a freelancer?

Fabio: There are basically three steps. First you'll be asked to go through a process that screens people to limit participation to those who are serious and motivated and whose identity and location we can verify.

Second, once you're in the system, you have a digital profile, like your resume. You can also upload a picture of yourself and examples of your work like images, web pages, writing samples, anything that is relevant.

The third stage is when you start to differentiate yourself. If it's relevant, we offer over 400 online skills tests you can take to show how you rank against everybody else that offers those same skills. Say we have a WordPress specialist who takes the test and ranks in the top one percent in the world on WordPress. That really helps him win more jobs. He has a much higher hourly rate than anybody else in his category because his test results are so high. So those are the kinds of things that you do to differentiate.

But you don't have to do all three steps, and you don't have to do them all at once. There are people who sign up and become active in half an hour, and others that go through the process and take a little bit more time.

Scott: If there are 500,000 contractors on the site, how does an individual compete? Are there differentiation strategies or marketing tips you could share for an individual who is looking to become a successful contractor?

Fabio: Start by deciding what set of skills you want to highlight. Don't try and position yourself as somebody who does everything well. That's not going to work. If you don't narrow your focus, you're going to come across as somebody who knows a little bit of a lot of things and therefore not much. It's best to say you have passion about something, and to build your profile around it. Pick examples that support what you're good at and upload those to your profile. Show your credentials, list the skills, and pick the keywords, all the things that make your profile discoverable on Elance. It's pretty easy to do.

Once you've created your profile, the next step is writing proposals. The biggest mistake you can make is to submit proposals that are not tailored to the specific project you are bidding on. People see right through that. If you haven't taken time to read the job post, and you can't write one sentence that is specific to why you think you can do a good job for that particular client, don't bother submitting a proposal.

Don't expect to apply for a job and get work right away. If you do, you're very lucky. We have plenty of people that have done that but the majority of people have to perfect the process. One thing we always hear from our successful freelancers is to keep doing it for a while and learn from your mistakes.

Scott: Can you share some success stories?

Fabio: There are tons. For example, Ben Gran from Iowa. He used to work full-time at a bank. He started working on Elance as a writer part-time for extra cash when his wife became pregnant. About a year in he quit his well-paid, prestigious job at the bank to work on Elance as a writer full-time. Now he's done dozens of projects and has a portfolio of clients from Tokyo to Australia to the UK. So he's a U.S.-midwest-based knowledge worker with a multinational business of one. It's a fascinating story.

Julie Babikan, from outside of Chicago, was working for a big accounting firm but was laid off unexpectedly. She could have spent her time looking for another job but instead she decided she wanted to gain control of her life. Little by little she started to build her own business. Now she has left the accounting world entirely and is making a full time living as a graphic designer with her own little agency.

I think people like this who to take their careers into their own hands are the heroes of our economy.

Scott: What I'm hearing are stories of people actually *reinventing* themselves by changing careers through freelance project work. You've got a banker who became a creative writer; you've got an accountant who became a graphic designer. That's exciting stuff not just from a financial point of view, but really from a *life* point of view.

Fabio: It doesn't work for everyone, but there are plenty of people that are able to do it.

ClickMillionaires.com Member Bonus: Listen to the rest of the interview with eLance CEO Fabio Rosati anytime on ClickMillionaires.com. You'll hear more of his suggestions on the best ways to market yourself to

attract work, how to validate and expand your credentials, how to make sure
you get paid, and how to build a profitable business doing freelance projects.

How to Reinvent Yourself Through Freelancing

If you have skills you'd like to put to work in your after-hours or on
weekends, or if you want to start building a practice of your own
around a new skill set, offering your services through project marketplaces online is a great place to do it. This kind of work makes money
from client payments, usually on a per-project or hourly basis. If you
have valuable preexisting expertise you can likely charge rates that
exceed $100/hour, while more widely available skills generally bill at
$10/hour or less. As you build a track record of satisfied clients, you'll
be able to gradually raise your rates, as well as discover the kinds of
projects you like the best in order to develop more specialized,
higher-paying skills.

While building your expertise and enhancing your track record
you can avoid the hassle, the responsibility, and many of the administrative requirements of starting a formal business by working for
others through an online service like Elance.com. They handle all
the billing, timesheets, and collections for you and it's free to use.
You figure out which kinds of projects you like and you only bid on
those that will continue to excite you even after you come home from
a long day at work.

You can design your life and redesign your career using this strategy. Perhaps you can build a business around transcription or customer service, or sales or writing or video editing or programming,
or maybe you're a lawyer or an aspiring designer. All those different
skills can be put to use on different projects. As you build more skills
and develop a track record, you can raise your rates and redesign
your life around work you love while getting paid to do it.

Even if you have no specific skills, you can act as a virtual assistant and work remotely to help other people run their business. Using email and Skype, cheap telephone services, and all the online tools we have today, telecommuting to do this sort of work is easier than ever. You might start at only 5 or 10 bucks an hour, but if you do your projects well consistently over time, you can get your rates up. There are people making $50 an hour, $80 an hour, $100 an hour. I went and looked at some of those examples that Fabio gave in our interview and one of the guys has done over 3,000+ projects on Elance alone and grossed over $700,000.

Freelancing Can Be Your Entry Point to a New Career and Lifestyle

Now I know freelancing is not the answer for everybody. But I wanted to include this section because a lot of you have been reading my books and blog, listening to my podcasts, watching my videos on YouTube, or maybe even tried ClickMillionaires.com, but you still feel there is something not quite right in your life. You want to make a move, you know the Internet is the place to make that move, but you don't know where to start.

Most of the emphasis online is that you need to come up with your own idea and then build that into a company. I'm still a big fan of that approach and that's where I'd like to see you end up. But starting as a part-time freelance contractor may be your *entry point* to profitable self-employment, with a lot less risk than starting your own company.

Becoming a freelance contractor can be a great way to get paid to learn about the aspects of e-business that interest you. It can be like a scholarship to go to college because other people will pay you while you're learning. This might mean taking smaller jobs than you had in mind when you started, but you've got to walk before you can run.

If "analysis paralysis" has got you by the throat, and you're not sure where to start, testing the waters as an independent contractor might be a winning get-started approach for you.

Freelancing is a little different from my normal Click Millionaires approach, but it's an opportunity for you. It's up to you how much you work, and what kind of projects you pick. But if you explore and learn and get paid along the way, you might be able change careers or even reinvent yourself around a Click Millionaire lifestyle business that you love.

Profitable Virtual Assistant Strategies

You don't have to be a programmer or have advanced expertise to become a well-paid specialist employed "virtually" today. Just basic computer skills and a professional manner can be the foundation for a virtual assistant business of your own. A "Virtual Assistant" is simply an assistant who works remotely, like from a home office, rather than in the same office as the boss. Virtual assistants make money helping larger businesses with everything from trivial administrative tasks to major marketing campaigns. Over the past 10 years they have become a cost-effective alternative to having an assistant in the office.

When virtual assistants first appeared on the scene, they mostly just handled traditional administrative assistant type duties like scheduling meetings, correspondence, travel arrangements, answering phones, etc. But with email and the cheap telephone service offered by the Internet, they quickly became cost-effective helpers to executives and business owners worldwide. Today the duties of VAs have evolved to almost any kind of work that can be done online, from e-mail correspondence to research, social media marketing to PR campaigns, and more.

Virtual assistants are freelancers, but they usually get paid more, and more consistently (often on a monthly retainer basis). Many VAs have years of office experience as administrative assistants (or even as executives themselves) but that's not required. If you know how to behave professionally in business settings, then you can become a virtual assistant, too.

To market their services, most VAs participate in project marketplaces when looking for new clients but they also post more detailed information about their skills and preferred types of work on a personal website. There they can post a pricing page offering their services at a base hourly rate and also in discounted "packages" that offer preset numbers of hours usually paid on a monthly retainer basis. These rates commonly start at minimum wage (or below for VAs based outside the United States) but $80 or even $100/hour is not uncommon for VAs with specific expertise. Here's an example:

Base Hourly Rate $35/hour	**Package 1** 10 Hours/month For $315 (10% savings)	**Package 2** 20 Hours/month For $560 (20% savings)

The fun parts of virtual assistant work are that it offers so many of the lifestyle benefits Click Millionaires like: flexible schedules, working from home, and a diversity of topics and people to work with, plus the more stable income of monthly retainer money. As a VA you can enjoy being part of a company's team and help build businesses, but without the costs and commute of working in the same office.

18

copycat millionaires (and billionaires!)

KRISTOF LINDNER is an engineer who was stuck in an office job in Germany but had his eyes on bigger things. He found a popular self-help course online from the United States and wondered why it wasn't available in German. In the evenings and on weekends after his "real job" he worked to translate and import it to Germany. Three years later Kristof has a seven-figure business and has expanded to six more active sites, too, several of which are based on licensing popular digital products from the United States.

▸   ▸   ▸

Have you have read this far but inspiration still has not struck you?

There's another proven way to make money online—imitate an already successful online business! Copying website business models, services, or design from one industry to another, or across international borders, offers you huge Click Millionaire opportunities. Of course, I don't mean that you should rip off an existing business. But repurposing a successful business model by refocusing its target market or repurposing proven valuable types of content into new formats can be a great way to get started.

A business that has already made it has proved that there is demand for its services. If you mimic one, you are saving yourself lots of expensive and time-consuming market research and product development. You can imitate small features that you see on other websites, mimic layout and design, or build a full-scale imitation of the business model.

The most impressive example of this approach is provided by the Samwer brothers of Germany. Marc, Oliver, and Alexander Samwer have become billionaires by importing and imitating successful online businesses from the United States. They started by building the first German eBay-style copycat site back in 1999. Just four months later, eBay bought it for $50 million in stock.

After that huge success, the Samwers kept going. They started a ringtone company called Jamba and sold that to Verisign for $273 million. Then they invested in a German Facebook clone that was sold for $100 million in 2007. They also expanded into investing in U.S. companies including Facebook and LinkedIn, which has given them even more cash to invest in start-ups, especially those interested in expanding to or from Europe. More recently they created a German Groupon-style site and managed to sell it to Groupon in just five months.

As the Samwers' success demonstrates, most site imitations emerge overseas because the original English-language sites aren't as useful to locals there. It also helps that local intellectual property laws usually offer less protection to the original sites founders than in the United States. For example, more than a thousand clones of Groupon appeared in China alone soon after its launch.

Creating Your Own "Copycat" Business System

You don't have to look to foreign markets for these kinds of opportunities, however. If you find a winning business strategy there are many ways to repurpose it for your own profit. Competing can be difficult and expensive if you're trying to break into capital-intensive industries like automobiles or online search (where Ford and Google both spend billions on engineering talent and infrastructure).

But starting new websites is much less risky, less expensive, and can allow you to serve niche interests more profitably. Many already popular Web companies have grown so big that they are no longer serving niche needs particularly well and are ready for niche competition.

For example, eBay dominates auctions but is there room for an online auction service that you could start that is focused just on a passion, community, or product that interests you? Maybe an auction service for cat toys and grooming equipment? Or an auction service only for used office furniture, hockey collectibles, or only-used-once wedding dresses?

Maybe there's a general blog that everybody in your industry reads. But you could start a new one that focuses only on people in that industry who work at a certain big company, or in a specific geographic region, or the international employees of a U.S. company, or a podcast for any of those.

Directories are also fairly easy to start. There are plenty of them already for general topics but maybe you could start a listings service only for preschools that teach French, dentists in Georgia, or used Cadillac parts suppliers in Canada.

Or, how about:

▸ Reformatting a winning content or service strategy into a new delivery vehicle, like turning a popular blog into a podcast, or an email newsletter into a e-book or video series?

▸ Writing a noozle or blog dedicated to covering news in just one chosen industry (like Al Peterson's NTS Media Online, discussed in Chapter 9) or only about one MLM company that you like?

▸ Creating an online video show or series about makeup tips as the Fowler sisters have done successfully on YouTube (Chapter 12)—but in Spanish, Russian, or Chinese?

▸ Updating previous ideas to new media and delivery methods. For example, CraigsList killed newspaper classifieds by offering similar services posted on Web pages. What proven services or info can you offer to take advantage of new mobile capabilities?

▸ Mixing and matching: If you find a target market you like, you can look at existing competitors' sites that address that market already. Pick and choose the best features of each to create a remix of your own that might combine the content approach of one with the sales model of another and the social media marketing or community-building tricks of a third.

These kinds of creative approaches offer opportunities for Click Millionaires to imitate pieces of proven bigger businesses and serve their niche customers better. Look at the personal interests you identified in the exercises in Part One. Look at services you like or imagined ones that you wish existed. The key again is identifying customer demand and problems that you can solve. Then work backward to find the easiest and most appealing way to deliver solutions to that audience profitably.

Cashing In on Proven Business Models

Your site could be bought—even before it starts attracting lots of traffic—if it proves audience demand for your new version or reinvention of an already popular service. This is how the Samwer brothers have made most of their money—they start new sites that serve the needs of the local audience and soon find the original site owners knocking on their door with a (very large) checkbook.

"Daily deals" websites have been the latest craze for copycats to profit from. Groupon has been on a buying spree, purchasing imitators in Russia, Japan, Germany, and Chile. And DailyDeal.de, a Groupon clone launched in Berlin in 2009, was acquired by Google. The brothers who founded it, Fabian and Ferry Heilemann, sold the company for an estimated $100 million plus as much as $50 million more in future earnings.

You can do this, too. Maybe you don't have the technology background to imitate some of these higher-tech examples, but you also probably don't need $150 million to lead a life you are happy about.

How to Clone a Successful Website to Create Your Own Business

To build your own version of an already successful site, you can use the popular Web-based site-building services discussed in later chapters to get started quickly and inexpensively Or, if you have already proved the demand for your new venture and are ready to spend some money to build the "real thing," head over to the project marketplaces discussed in Chapter 17. You can post a project request that details the type of website that you want built. You'll soon get bids from freelance developers all over the world offering to help you realize your vision.

PART FIVE
HOW TO FIND YOUR
NICHE ON THE INTERNET

The secret of success is making your vocation your vacation. —Mark Twain, author

You may feel like you have nothing to say or not enough expertise to build a business upon, but I think you do. Look around your own life. You are likely a member of many overlapping "insider" groups. Your job, former jobs, your industry, where you went to school, your family, your neighborhood, your favorite sports teams or hobbies, your kids or relatives, your ethnic background, your religion, your political affiliations, the charities you support, the medical issues faced by you or your family members, your insurance, dining, travel, decorating, or gardening needs, etc. All of your daily activities add up to personal expertise in various subcultures—probably without you even realizing it.

We also live at a unique time in history—when retail marketing is fragmenting into niches and old media is losing its grip on the audience's attention. Consumers and businesses worldwide are resetting their media consumption and buying habits in radical new ways. The result of these fundamental changes is the blossoming of millions of small flowers of niche opportunity for you to build a lifestyle business system of your own, drawing upon your own life's experiences and interests. Online you can pull together customers whose common interests are underserved and fill their demand with helpful, profitable products that also help you improve your lifestyle.

Your challenge today is to find a niche like this that you like and grow an audience there before the competition does. If you do, you'll have a huge head start on your way to a Click Millionaire lifestyle business.

The key is to get started *today*.

· · · · · · 19 · · · · · · ·

collect attention to build a profitable niche audience

TODAY WE'RE all busy and getting busier. There are more products and more information trying to grab our attention than ever before. To succeed today your venture, product, or content needs to clearly answer customers' fundamental question: "Is this worth my time?"

In the 20th century you had to visit a store to shop. And that store had a large, long-term investment in buildings, equipment, staff, marketing, and the distribution relationships needed to supply its inventory. Meanwhile, media production was largely restricted to professionals who worked for big newspaper, broadcasting, or publishing companies. But today all of those retailers and media businesses are fighting for their lives against low-cost Internet-based retailers and amateur content providers. Plus, there are distractions like video games, Facebook, and mobile devices (and video games played on Facebook on our mobile devices!) that keep people out of stores and distracted.

Profiting in the New Attention Economy

Today audience demand is more important than product supply so finding your audience is the most important part of developing your Click Millionaire business. Don't make the mistake of looking for products to sell first. Focusing on supply is the old way of starting a business from the days when distribution was difficult. It can cost you thousands of dollars and leave you with a garage full of unwanted product samples if you don't get it exactly right the first time. The Internet now makes almost any product or information quickly available. So you should invest your start-up time in finding people you can help, needs you can fill, problems you can solve—and building an audience around serving that customer demand.

To do all that, your website needs to be better. And "better" today means appealing more precisely to customer niche interests than mainstream media and retailers can. But you'd better hurry up. There are only so many hours in every customer's day and only so many customers available. So your first challenge is not to find or create the perfect product—it's to collect *attention*. If you can build a customer audience, you can make money online from almost any topic, from aardvarks to microbiology to zippers. What you need is to identify ways to serve the needs of your chosen groups of readers, listeners, or participants with your own content, product, or community system. Then you can make money through a combination of online advertising sales, e-commerce product sales, subscriptions, and anything else you can dream up that interests them.

Start building your audience today because if you start now when nobody is watching, you can make mistakes and have fun building your website and experimenting in social media. It's also easier to make friends before the pressure is on and those friendships can spark the long-term relationships you need to build a long-term business success. And, by starting small and casual, you can learn along the way what's most important to your audience so you can serve them better and more profitably. Plus, if you try to catch up later, it's expensive! You will be faced with more competitors and likely have to buy your way into the market with expensive advertising.

Don't Think It's Too Late for You

It might sound crazy to you that today, even after 15+ years of Internet business growth, that there are still niche markets available for you to profit from online. But since my first book, *Internet Riches*, was published in 2006, more multi-billion-dollar online businesses have blossomed than I can count. YouTube, Facebook, Twitter, Zynga, Groupon, etc. All of these websites seemingly came out of nowhere in recent years to collect hundreds of millions of users (and billions of dollars in valuation). And those are just the big names everyone has heard of—imagine how many smaller entrepreneurs have found six-, seven-, and eight-figure success online in recent years, too.

Online advertising, e-commerce, international expansion, and especially mobile technologies are all combining to create new business opportunities for you as you read this. Even after 20 years of commercial growth the Internet still only attracts 15 percent of total ad spending in the United States, and only 8 percent of U.S. retail sales.[1] That clearly allows room for billions more dollars to flow to online businesses like yours!

The Internet allows people to communicate across boundaries of time, place, and increasingly even language. This allows them to find each other and share rare pursuits, specialized topics, and niche activities that were previously isolated from each other. This creates new, niche markets for you to tap, especially if you can create services, products, or communities that help serve the previously underserved needs of these groups or give them places to meet one another. The challenge is finding an area where the audience is underserved that interests you so much personally that you are inspired to build a business around it.

Why I Like Niches

Niche interests and subcultures offer the best places for you to look for potential customers. Here's why:

- There is less competition in niches so you can more quickly attract an audience and get on your way to making money.

- The people who populate each niche tend to be enthusiastic about it. This can save you tons of money in marketing because those people already know other people who share their similar niche interests. If you do a good job serving them, they'll tell their friends. In the age of the Internet, that kind of word-of-mouth marketing is extremely cost-effective.

- If you pick a niche you like, you can find yourself enjoying your work more than ever before. That's the point of Click Millionaire lifestyle businesses.

- And, last, niches are really all that's left. The big, obvious business opportunities online have mostly filled up. And any big new ones that emerge are quickly pounced upon by venture capital–backed teams with strong experience, technical

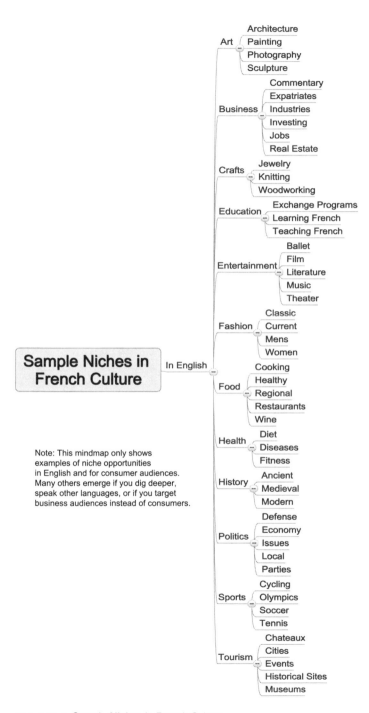

Note: This mindmap only shows
examples of niche opportunities
in English and for consumer audiences.
Many others emerge if you dig deeper,
speak other languages, or if you target
business audiences instead of consumers.

Figure 19–1. Sample Niches in French Culture

skills, and connections. You don't need to compete against those guys. Building something smaller that you like to serve a niche you enjoy can be a perfectly good recipe for a profitable lifestyle business of your own.

Examples of Market Niches

Don't dismiss any category that interests you—*today the riches are in niches*. There is lots of business opportunity still available in subcategories that deserve more specialized services and products.

Figure 19–1 shows how even a seemingly niche topic like French culture can be broken down into many smaller sub niches. Each of these sub niches has its own audience potential that could support the Click Millionaires who build businesses there first.

Here are a few other examples of niches just to show you how to think about markets that may interest you:

Major Market > Market > Sub Market > Niche > Sub Niche

- Health > Disease > Diabetes > Juvenile Diabetes > Juvenile Diabetes in Canada

- Aerospace > Airplanes > Jets > Jet Air Shows >Jet Air Show Staff

- Education > High School > Foreign Exchange Student Programs > Foreign Exchange Student Programs from Russia

- Real Estate > Residential Real Estate > Rental Investment Properties > Rentals in Texas > Vacation Rentals on the Texas Coast

- Sports > Cricket > Pakistani Cricket Fans > Pakistani Cricket Fans living in the USA

> **CLICK MILLIONAIRES SECRET: Make the First
> Dollar First!**
>
> *Start by focusing on your most likely path for generating revenue the soon-
> est so you can see your efforts rewarded and pay some bills. If your great
> idea requires 100,000 users before you start making money, you are setting
> yourself up for failure. Instead, make the first dollar first. Then make two dol-
> lars. Grow your way up to making several dollars at a time but built on a busi-
> ness system you design that requires as little work from you as possible.*
>
> *Don't go broke trying to pursue ideas that are too big or long-term at first.
> It will be a lot easier to pursue those ideas once you have income instead of
> spreading yourself too thin now before you have any revenue at all.*

To find potentially profitable small business niches (and avoid too much competition), you often need to dig four or five levels deep.

Money Is Not Your Only Goal

When evaluating your potential business niches, you'll need to balance money against lifestyle considerations.

Yes, how much money you can make is a top consideration. But don't forget the Lifestyle Design Shopping List you developed in Chapter 4. It's right there in your Click Millionaires Idea Journal. As you redesign your life, you have an unprecedented opportunity to build your lifestyle goals into the daily operations of the new business you are creating for yourself.

Both current and recurring revenue from product sales or ads is your goal. Ideally your niche will also enable you to create a sales "ladder" of progressively more expensive upsell products that bring in additional revenue from your most loyal audience members over time.

CHAPTER 19 NOTE

The Internet: Older, Wiser, Plenty Of Upside, Says Barclays; http://blogs.barrons.com/techtraderdaily/2011/09/16/the-internet-older-wiser-plenty-of-upside-says-barclays/

the click millionaires business niche identification method

In order to help you identify a profitable and enjoyable lifestyle business niche for yourself, below is my nine-step "Click Millionaires Method." Take some time to work through the process below. I think you'll quickly see that you have unique experience and perspectives to share with others when designing your new lifestyle business. Be sure to get out your Click Millionaires Idea Journal to record your answers to these business design exercises.

Nine Steps to Finding Your Niche on the Internet

To help you develop a Click Millionaires business system personalized to your interests, here are the nine steps of the Click Millionaires

Business Niche Identification Method (see Figure 20–1) to help you identify the best niche market for your own lifestyle business.

STEP 1: START WITH THE FOUR Ps

To start your personalized niche identification process, choose one of the following Four Ps: *Passion, People, Problem,* or *Product* as the foundation for your new lifestyle business.

> **PASSION *NICHE BUSINESS MODEL IDENTIFICATION:*** If you think that you'd like to develop a business around a hobby, passion, issue, or industry, start looking at your own personal interests, hobbies, expertise, a "calling" you have to pursue, a message you feel you need to share, a business area where you have special expertise, or a cause you feel is important to promote.

> **PEOPLE *NICHE BUSINESS MODEL IDENTIFICATION:*** Think about the kind of people you most like to spend time with. Building your own lifestyle business serving them will give you even more time together, so start by looking at your own background, education, family roots, or hobbies to identify people you'd like to work with more. Almost any interest that you share with other people can be the basis of a new business audience for you online today. Who are the people you would most like to help?

> **PROBLEM *NICHE BUSINESS MODEL IDENTIFICATION:*** Look at the needs, inefficiencies, and inconveniences you see in your own daily life. Wherever there's a problem, there's need for solutions that your Click Millionaire business may be able to make money solving. Start with identifying customer problems. Then work toward providing solutions through your new business. Bottom line: Is there a way you can make life more convenient for people?

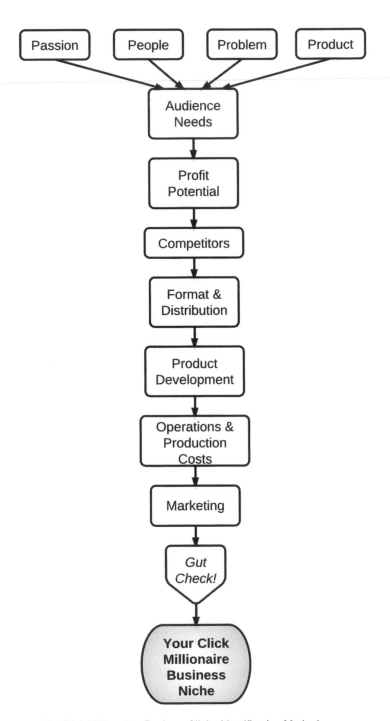

Figure 20–1. The Click Millionaires Business Niche Identification Method

PRODUCT *NICHE BUSINESS MODEL IDENTIFICATION:* Look at your own business or life to find a product that deserves a wider audience. You might be inspired to create one yourself. Or maybe you have products or services or information already available that you want to market.

To help determine which of the Four Ps (Passion, People, Problem, or Product) you want to use as the starting point for your new business, don't forget to look back at your Click Millionaires Idea Journal for the results of your lifestyle design brainstorming exercises from Chapter 4. Draw upon the Lifestyle Design Shopping List likes and dislikes you brainstormed there to help identify which of the Four Ps is the best starting place for you. Once Step 1 has helped you determine a good starting point for finding your Click Millionaire business niche, you can proceed through the following steps.

> **CLICK MILLIONAIRES SECRET: Just Brainstorm— Don't Judge (Yet!)**
>
> *Take all the time you need to identify the opportunities that best fit your Lifestyle Design Shopping List and also offer the best opportunity for profitability. Spending time to find a niche that truly interests you will pay off both financially and by letting you redesign your life around a business you actually enjoy! Don't jump to conclusions about your ideas yet, either. Go ahead and be creative. We'll do some helpful business analysis later to help keep you from wasting your time.*
>
> *Allocate at least 10 pages of your Click Millionaires Idea Journal purely for scribbling down ideas you have that answer these Four Ps niche brainstorming questions.*

STEP 2: AUDIENCE NEEDS ANALYSIS

Next look at the needs of the audience that your chosen Passion, People, Problem, or Product topic attracts. How can you best help your audience? As you saw in Click Millionaires Success Principle #1

(Chapter 5), determining how you can help others is the foundation of most great businesses. Starting with the people who share your passion or have the problems you want to target, what are their top needs that your e-business could make money by serving?

STEP 3: PROFIT POTENTIAL

Evaluate your target market's size and the needs and purchasing power of the potential customers in that market. Does this audience spend money on the products, services, or information you propose to offer? Looking at the needs you've listed in the previous step, will those customers pay money for you to help them? If so, are there products already available that you can sell? Or will advertisers pay for you to promote their products to the people who visit your website?

STEP 4: COMPETITORS ANALYSIS

Look at similar sites to see what is working to serve needs similar to those you are targeting. The marketplace will show you what works if you look. Don't look only at direct competitors but also at similar products/services in other markets. What are those sites offering? Do you like what they are doing or do you think your website could do better? Is the content cool, appropriate, or targeted enough to serve the niche well? You don't need to reinvent the wheel, especially at first. Take the "best of" the similar sites you can find to design your own business model and products. Among the potential competitors you identify, what can you do that's different enough that people will want to read your blog, watch your videos, buy your e-books, etc?

> **CLICK MILLIONAIRES SECRET: Respect Competition but Don't Fear It**
> The mere existence of competitors does not mean you can't succeed! Don't stop your brainstorming because you're worried about competitors. Every big market has at least three to five players. Yes, the top one gets most of the

business—but the others are still making money or they wouldn't still be around! Being second, or even fifth, can make for a fine Click Millionaire lifestyle business.

STEP 5: FORMAT AND DISTRIBUTION ANALYSIS

The format you choose to deliver your content can have a huge effect on your success, even with the same content. A blog attracts a different audience than a podcast or video, for example. So given the audience needs you identified above, what's the best way to reach your audience? You might consider the following formats:

- blogs

- forums

- noozles

- podcasts

- videos

- teleseminars

- mobile apps

The "best" format for your Click Millionaire business is the one that your targeted audience prefers. So, where do your customers spend time and how do they prefer to consume info?

STEP 6: PRODUCT DEVELOPMENT

Package up your research, lifestyle redesign priorities, and ideas into a few of your best guesses at the new "product" you'll create. Which items, services, or concepts offer you the best opportunities to make money and also to include your Lifestyle Design Shopping List priorities in your daily operations? Test each of those concepts against the remaining questions in these exercises to see how they perform.

Sharpen your focus on helping people by providing specific solutions to their problems. You want to be selling aspirin (a "must have"), not vitamins (just a "nice to have").

STEP 7: OPERATIONS AND PRODUCTION COSTS ANALYSIS

With each of the business ideas you have developed so far, estimate answers to the following questions:

- How much of your time and money will your new venture take to start?

- What are the recurring operating costs?

- Does the website, content, marketing, or product itself require regular updating?

- How much of the production can be automated with software? (Click Millionaires Success Principle #3)

- Can you hire people to replace yourself or does operation require your personal involvement? (Click Millionaires Success Principle #4)

- Can you design the business so that the audience contributes as much of the content as possible? (Click Millionaires Success Principle #5)

- If the business starts to succeed, will it scale by itself or require additional resources of time or money to serve more customers? (Click Millionaires Success Principle #6)

- Will growth increase profitability or hurt it?

These are "make-or-break" questions that can help you separate profitable opportunities from daydreams. Also, I'd rather you avoid raising money from outside investors, so calculating your start-up and day-to-day operating costs is important to determine if you can launch your new business ideas independently.

STEP 8: MARKETING ANALYSIS

Finding cost-effective ways to reach your target customers is a critical part of any business plan. Luckily you have the Internet making it easier than ever for you to reach new customers. Even better is that the Internet allows your customers to tell their friends about your business using social media tools like Facebook, Twitter, Google+, blogs, review sites, etc. Building your business so that you offer plenty of free info and perks worth sharing is a good strategy today. That can help attract new customers and encourage them to spread the word online cheaply for you. Look closely at competitors' marketing strategies. Try to identify holes in their marketing approaches that your new business can fill to differentiate itself and reach your target market cost-effectively. Remember, product supply is not the hard part anymore. Online today it's the customer demand that you need to find and cultivate.

(For a more in-depth look at modern marketing strategies, social media, SEO, and audience attraction techniques, try the Click Millionaires video training course at www.TrafficBuildingSchool.com or read my book, *e-Riches 2.0: Next Generation Online Marketing Strategies* (AMACOM, 2009). Both are full of friendly recommendations in plain English on how to attract more customers to your website using cost-effective modern marketing strategies like email, blogging, social networks, podcasting, online video and even public relations.)

STEP 9: THINK AND DECIDE FOR YOURSELF (GUT CHECK!)

If I had asked my customers what they wanted, they simply would have said a faster horse.
—attributed to Henry Ford, founder of the Ford Motor Company

Your goal is to identify an audience of people you'd like to hang out with that has strong and recurring needs, and then to make a system out of serving those needs well enough that you make money while still enjoying yourself and your new work. But all the analysis in the world won't necessarily produce the right answer for your personal situation.

Now that you're "the boss," your first decision as CEO is to make the big decision about where to focus your energy. You'll need to balance different factors to make the challenging choice of which of your new lifestyle business ideas to pursue first. The lifestyle business you build should be more reflective of who you are and your personal goals than any set of spreadsheets can tell you.

If you want to build a Click Millionaire lifestyle business for yourself, you need to start thinking for yourself, doing your own research, running your own numbers, and investing your own time and money to make it happen. If you'd like more help with this important decision, download the expanded e-book version of "The Click Millionaires Method for Business Niche Identification." It includes dozens more pages and specific step-by-step questions to help you through each part of the niche identification process in more depth. It's available once you register at ClickMillionaires.com.

Niche Mathematics: The Click Millionaires Success Formula

More important than the size of your niche audience is their interest in what you are saying and selling. So a big audience with casual interest may have less revenue and profit potential than a small audience if that smaller audience is more interested and involved. This audience "engagement level" leads directly to revenue because it expresses how interested your fans are in buying your products, recruiting their friends, and returning to your site regularly to click on your ads.

If you put that idea into a mathematical-style equation, it looks like this:

Size of Audience × Revenue per Audience Member based on Engagement Level = Potential Revenue

If you have 100,000 fans in your audience, and they are engaged at a low level that might generate just $1/year of purchases or ad clicks per audience member, that creates a $100,000 business for you.

Other ways to build yourself a $100,000 a year business could include:

10,000 fans × moderate engagement of $10 revenue per fan per year = $100,000/year business for you

1,000 fans × strong engagement of $100 per fan per year = $100,000/year business for you

100 fans × very strong engagement of $1,000 per fan per year = $100,000/year business for you

As you can see, the two keys are the size of the audience and their level of engagement in your content and products. The Law of Large Numbers is a financial lesson I learned in my first career as a Wall Street investment banker and discussed in my first book, *Internet Riches* (AMACOM, 2006). It states: "A little number multiplied by a big number is still a big number." Banks use this math to collect tiny percentages of all the very large transactions they handle, generating billions of dollars in profit every year. In a Click Millionaires context the "large number" you need to make money online can be either the *quantity* of your audience or the *quality* of a small audience that is highly engaged because your products, content, or ads fit their needs.

If you can attract both a large audience and get them really engaged, your niche math might look like this:

10,000 fans × very strong engagementment of $1,000 per fan per year = $10,000,000 annually!

As the owner of your own Click Millionaire business you can choose to attract a high quantity of website visitors or to increase engagement quality from a smaller group. You can control the audience you attract by varying the marketing, products, content, and pricing you offer.

Market Sizing: Find a Big Opportunity
but Keep Your Company Small

Now that you see the Click Millionaires Success Formula, you can use it to evaluate potential business approaches for yourself. For example, if you're looking at diet products online, you can see that they are often very successful because they rank highly on both of the variables in the Formula: Big audiences (everybody wants to lose weight) and high engagement (losing weight is very personal and also a recurring need). This adds up to big money for those who succeed with diet products. Unfortunately that success also means tons of competition in popular niches like dieting. So your goal is to find a niche target market with lots of audience potential but fewer competitors.

Don't bite off a bigger niche than you can chew. When deciding what kind of audience to focus on, I encourage you to be ambitious but also to be smart. It's tempting to "go big" and target a large, broad market but most big and obvious market opportunities are already busy by now. You need to be smarter and identify opportunities that the "big boys" have not seen yet or think are too small to pursue.

On the other hand, you don't want to go too small either. When I say "find a niche" it's common for new members of our Click Millionaires.com community to pick niches that are too small to make any money. Often they are so worried about competition, wasting their time, or insecure about their own business skills that they limit themselves to an already comfortable and familiar target market. This is most common where they have limited themselves (and their audience size) by geography. Focusing on small audiences like those interested in home sales in just one neighborhood, students at just one elementary school, parishioners at one local church, an alumni association for a small college, or a sports team with a limited following are all examples of this.

These audiences are fun and interesting but they are inherently limited in size because they target only a small group of people to start. If there are only 300 houses in that neighborhood, or only 500 people attending that school, church, or team games, you'll need every family, local homeowner, or team fan to buy an unlikely amount of your stuff to make any money.

While these types of target markets can be great places to test your concept, you'll also want to think ahead to how you can grow to attract larger audiences that will generate more sales and/or lots of traffic to your advertisers. So as your business grows maybe you can expand your real estate site to include more ZIP codes or add services like plumbers, gardeners, and insurance brokers that interest your audience of homeowners. Or for the other examples, maybe you expand your website to offer news from other schools or churches in the area or sports updates for the whole league instead of just your favorite team.

> **CLICK MILLIONAIRES SECRET: The Easiest Audiences**
> The easiest audiences to recruit into your online business system are those that have recurring reasons to interact (like preexisting real-world communities) that are also geographically dispersed. These groups are natural users of the Internet so that they can keep in touch easily and across time zones. Give them a platform to interact on, or products and information that serve their specialized needs and they will reward you.

Experts Can't Believe This Kind of Success

As you begin to settle on your lifestyle business niche, you'll likely start to doubt your own choices. Naysayers in your life will deny the potential of anything that they don't understand, too.

But traditional definitions of corporate success don't apply to Click Millionaire businesses. Business school professors overlook them because they don't have lots of employees to manage and bankers prefer to focus on big corporations since they have more capital. The professors and bankers dismiss "lifestyle businesses" with a judgmental smirk, ignoring the fact that your lifestyle is *the #1 concern* in your life!

It's your job to see past their mental limitations and recognize that even a business that generates only $1,000 a month is still very worth it if that $1,000 a month comes in on an automated, recurring basis with little work on your part.

Because you can reach so many people and share information and digital products so inexpensively with the worldwide activity of the Internet, it's possible today to build businesses with few or zero employees around niches that are small by traditional business standards.

And, since it's online, your new business has the potential to be seen by billions of people. With the right product mix and good marketing, even a tiny percentage of those potential customers could make you a Click Millionaire.

CLICK MILLIONAIRES SECRET: The Myth of the "Genius Idea"

You don't need to be a genius with a breakthrough idea to make money online. The media glorifies the Mark Zuckerbergs and Steve Jobs of the online world, but there are far more fortunes made simply improving previous ideas than creating new ones from scratch. For example, Facebook was not a completely original idea. Audience interest in socializing online existed long before the company started. Its success is built upon many preceding social networks, forums, mailing lists, and websites. Facebook just used newly available tools and connectivity to meet its audiences needs better. Google was not the first search engine either. It builds on the success of previous search engine companies but serves the search audience's need better than predecessors.

You may be impatient to conquer the world with a game-changing new idea. But not doing everything right away doesn't mean you're never going to get to do it! I would rather see you overwhelm a small niche, especially when getting started, than spread yourself too thin against tough competition. Establishing a foundation of moderate success from which you can expand is far more important than conquering the world from the very start. If you bite off too much, you'll run out of money, time, and patience before you have really "made it." Most success stories are based more on consistent daily execution and successful satisfaction of customers needs than on the unique "stroke of genius" that most people associate with entrepreneurial success.

Your Unique Service and Purpose (USP)

The overarching point in all this niche identification discussion is that you will win if you focus on helping people. We can brainstorm together, analyze the competition, crunch numbers, etc., but demand is the key. Helping others ease their burdens, make more money, feel better, or enjoy life more is usually a winning strategy. To emphasize the importance of this I'd like to introduce you to my (re)definition of the business school term "USP."

USP usually stands for "unique selling proposition." But instead of worrying about what you can *sell*, I'd like you to find your *Unique Service* and *Purpose*. How can you provide a service that others really need? What unique purpose are you here to serve? What is it about *you* that it's time to maximize and share with the world? And how can you put that together with the needs of others to provide a real service that helps other people, makes money, and makes a difference, too? These are really the ultimate questions that the previous exercises and my books are designed to help you uncover.

Only you can answer these questions, both intellectually and through your daily actions but the ClickMillionaires.com community and I are ready to help you. It's time to commit to something more than watching TV, trying to lose weight, and making money. What's next for you? How can you become the you that you want and deserve to be? You only get one shot at this life. It's not a dress rehearsal. What are you going to do with the days you have?

· · · · · · · 21 · · · · · · ·

testing customer demand before you waste your time

A good plan implemented today is better than a perfect plan implemented tomorrow.
—General George Patton

THIS BOOK IS dedicated to making sure that you profitably invest your time finding or creating products for an audience that wants them. Hopefully the previous chapters have helped you to develop not just cool ideas or new ways to spend your time, but also products, services, and systems that are so valuable to your target customers that they will *pay you* for them. To help make certain that your new theories about audience demand prove out, this chapter shares several quick and low-cost ways to test your new business ideas with real people and do a simple financial analysis before you get in too deep. Testing is the best way to keep yourself from wasting time and money.

Use the tools detailed below to quickly collect information that can help you improve your products and profits. Especially when you are just starting out, getting feedback from real people is more important than making your product perfect. Websites and information products are easily updated and testing tools are widely available. There's no shame in launching a website or new products today, and later deciding they don't work. The software industry's gift to the modern business world is that you can just call projects like that "beta tests." Google does this all the time and you can, too.

New Business Idea Testing Tactics

Below are some quick and inexpensive ways to test your ideas.

‣ **Validate by talking to potential customers.** Don't just ask your friends and family what they think of your new business. They'll say what they think you want to hear because they love you. Instead, milk your potential customers and even competitors for information. For example, visit an online forum where your target customers hang out or even make some cold calls to potential customers in your niche to ask about their needs and your proposed product solutions. Most people are happy to answer a few simple questions if you are friendly and polite.

‣ **Run an online survey or poll.** Set up a simple online poll about your new products or website using a free tool like Vizu.com. Or run a more detailed survey like those quickly constructed online using SurveyMonkey.com. Share your questions by asking friends, family, and business acquaintances to forward the poll or survey to their network also. You can even allocate a small budget to pay per click (PPC) advertising to attract survey participants to increase your responses. Social media tools like Facebook, Twitter, and Google+ are also great for spreading the surveys beyond your personal circle for helpful but objective responses from people you don't know personally.

‣ **Validate with online keyword research.** Google AdWords offers an excellent Keyword Tool that's free to use. There you can type in the keywords for your website topic or product and, with a click of your mouse, the system will show you the number of searches for those keywords conducted on Google each day. For example, if you are selling mattresses, you can use this tool to enter words like "mattress," "mattresses," "box spring," etc. The Keyword Tool will instantly tell you that there are approximately 9,140,000 searches per month globally on the keyword "mattress" and approximately 5,000,000 searches locally.

Of course, you already know that mattresses are a popular product. The idea is for you to try this with your own keywords and see how many people are searching for what you think you might be selling. You'll want your products' keywords to attract a minimum of thousands of searches per month to show that there is audience interest. You can later use this info to help optimize your website to attract free search engine traffic, too.

Find Google's keyword tools and other helpful resources at www.GoogleKeywordsTool.com.

‣ **Check PPC advertising potential.** If your new business is going to try to make money from ads, you want to see how much pay-per-click (PPC) advertisers will pay for ads on sites that cover topics like yours. Here you can visit AdWords again but this time play the role of an advertiser. If you sign up for a free advertiser account you can test your keywords following the instructions in Chapter 23 to see what each ad click might be worth.

▸ **Get site design feedback.** Once you have your website designed, it's a good idea also to get feedback on its appearance. You may think your site is easy to use and pretty but real people might find it hard to use and distracting. Some good ways to get good design feedback are online:

- Usertesting.com, UsabilityHub.com, FiveSecondTest.com, and Usabilla.com offer usability testing and design feedback online. They have panels of real people quickly and inexpensively review websites.

- Unbounce.com helps you optimize your website landing pages. It does this by helping you easily create variations of the pages to see which ones attract the most clicks and convert the most visitors into buyers.

- ExpertWebSiteReviews.com is my personalized website video review service. Order a review and I will make a video for you of me personally reviewing the design, usability, SEO, layout, and product strategy of your website. It's an affordable, customized, and very helpful service that has attracted many happy client testimonials on the site and on my YouTube channel.

As you can see, getting customer feedback is a lot easier in the age of the Internet than it used to be!

> **CLICK MILLIONAIRES SECRET: Keep It Simple Stupid (K.I.S.S.)**
> The best new business ideas are simple: a simple idea in a simple wrapper that your target customers can quickly understand. Hearing about it should create a "light bulb moment" for anyone who hears of it. So don't get ahead of yourself—no one is interested in the third and fourth phases of your business's incredible potential until they clearly understand the start-up phase and how it benefits them.

Estimating Sales

Now let's try a simple numbers analysis to help you compare some of your business ideas to one another on a financial basis. Even if you hate math and are completely making up the numbers, rest assured that all entrepreneurs do exactly that when they start. An educated guess will still tell you a lot more than no calculation at all.

Let's try estimating your potential revenues using that Click Millionaires Success Formula from the earlier "Niche Mathematics" section in the previous chapter:

Size of Audience × Revenue per Audience Member based on Engagement Level = Potential Revenue

Plug in numbers for each of the blanks below to see your lifestyle business idea in action. This quick math can help you guesstimate the potential of your new niche business.

YEAR 1 ESTIMATES:

_____ × _____ = _____
(size of audience)   ($ per fan based on engagement level)   (potential revenue)

Don't forget to factor in recurring revenues from subscription products! (Click Millionaires Success Principle #7)

Now for Year 2 add in additional audience growth or additional revenues from product or service extensions, upgrades, upsells, or recurring subscriptions that your business will likely grow to include.

YEAR 2 ESTIMATES:

_____ × _____ = _____
(size of audience)   ($ per fan based on engagement level + more products)   (potential revenue)

This additional money won't show up overnight, but if you are realistic in your assumptions that might be a good estimate of your revenues in your second year.

For Year 3, hopefully you can increase your audience size, your engagement level, your product lines and your advertising revenues, too:

YEAR 3 ESTIMATES:

$$\underline{\hspace{3cm}} \times \underline{\hspace{8cm}} = \underline{\hspace{3cm}}$$

(size of audience)   ($ per fan based on engagement level + more products)   (potential revenue)

How to Use These Sales Estimates

These rough calculations can help you predict the profit potential of various business approaches so you can more easily compare and choose between them. For example, if your most optimistic assumptions only allow for 1,000 loyal visitors in your audience and they are all cheapskates who at best will only buy an average of one dollar each of your products (or make one dollar's worth of ad clicks) annually, then you're looking at only $1,000 per year in revenue. That may be okay for Year 1 if you have plans that will ramp that revenue up in Years 2 and 3. But if not, then you likely have found only a nice hobby. If you want it to grow into a profitable lifestyle business you will need to make changes to your niche, products, or marketing plan.

As you can see "engagement level" is a proxy for many more complex revenue modeling tools. Rather than spending lots of time with financial models, however, your time is better spent working on your lifestyle redesign, niche identification, product development, and marketing plans. Developing winning strategies in those categories will get you farther than fancy spreadsheets.

Build a "Portfolio" of Businesses for Multiple Streams of Income

Part of the fun of being your own boss is getting to pursue your own business ideas. Having lots of ideas can be a problem when you work for someone else because most jobs require you to focus on only one project at a time. But as a Click Millionaire entrepreneur it's okay and even profitable and fun to have multiple businesses going simultaneously. What's more, you can build these new lifestyle businesses around your personal interests so you have a "portfolio" of ongoing projects, all of which you enjoy working on!

This is the Click Millionaires way—explore new niches and focus on each one long enough to get a new business system built that serves that market. Remember to make the first dollar first for each one. But once you start making money on a recurring and automated or outsourced basis, you can move on! You'll also want to step back and revisit previous projects to update and fine-tune them as you go to increase their profitability.

You can accommodate a variety of projects (and interests) this way. It also solves the terrible need that entrepreneurs have for pursuing new ventures constantly. Try giving yourself time lines to manage your distractions. For example: "For three months I'm going to build that new website about butterfly collecting, then I'll revisit the community I started for Volkswagen mechanics for one week, then in March I'll be ready to spend three weeks starting the blog for Italian cooks."

The Venture Capitalists' Success Secret

This may sound a bit crazy, but this "portfolio approach" is exactly how venture capitalists make their money. They invest money in a bunch of different start-ups. They don't expect all of their investments to make it (and neither should you). But if one of the companies in their investment portfolio succeeds, it not only can pay for the failed investments, it can make them rich.

Now I doubt you have millions of dollars to mimic the venture capitalists' approach, but what you have instead is your time and the very low costs of business start-up online today. So if you spread your bets over three or five or ten different projects, you actually can increase your chances of making money. I do this myself. I personally have between five and ten (or more) websites operating at all times, each at different stages of development. Some are small and generate only a few dollars each day from ads online, but they require no work or updating from me. Some are new (and may even be on their way to failing), while others are well-established and generate thousands of dollars/month. Added together, over time, I've built a portfolio of interesting, ethical, fun, online businesses that help people worldwide daily with only part-time involvement from me.

You can, too. You're an entrepreneurial success story waiting to happen!

Follow Your "Calling"

Do you have a "calling," a message that you feel you are destined to share with the world? If you do, then all the analysis in the world is not going to "prove" the viability of your approach. In fact, most analysis will tilt against the success of a venture that is more based on your heart than your head. Do I think you should pursue your calling anyway? Absolutely!

Numerical analysis can't quantify what is in your heart or validate your intuition.

You may still be crazy—but the wide, cheap reach of the Internet means that any message can be spread online today if you are truly dedicated to making it happen.

PART SIX

NUTS AND BOLTS: BUILDING YOUR
BUSINESS AND MAKING MONEY

22

click millionaires systems for production and operations

THERE ARE MANY, many services available online that claim to be able to help you make money. Unfortunately, most of them are in business to make money *from you* while you build your Click Millionaire business online. That's why I am so skeptical of anything high-priced or that's promoted by "gurus," especially if I have not tested it myself. I'd like to see you save your money and invest your time in a do-it-yourself approach instead. Once you've found a profitable niche and developed a winning business system to mine it, then you can invest your hard-earned capital in more expensive expansion projects. Until then I recommend the low-cost services detailed below to help you get started.

Recommended Vendors

The most convenient and affordable Internet business services are browser-based, meaning that you can access them online anytime through your Internet browser program instead of buying software that you install on your own PC's hard drive. By using services like these that are delivered online you can avoid having to invent, purchase, install, or maintain software yourself. This "cloud-based computing" approach—formerly known in industry lingo as "software as a service" (SAAS) or "application service providers" (ASPs)—allows you to:

▸ Use powerful corporate-level software programs that are hosted "in the cloud" (e.g., on remotely based servers).

▸ Pay low monthly or annual fees.

▸ Rely on the service to update the software and ensure compatibility and upgrades.

▸ Store your data securely on their servers.

▸ Take advantage of new features and enhancements without having to develop or install them yourself.

In fact, if you are a nontechnical entrepreneur, you'll find that you can stitch together almost any kind of web-based business service you can imagine by signing up for different publishing, email, storage, advertising, marketing, and payment systems online.

Here are links to some of my favorite resources including some helpful reviews, discussions, and recommendations at Click Millionaires.com:

Popular Website- and Blog-Building Tools

▸ Wordpress (www.wordpress.com)

- Site Build It (www.TrySiteBuildIt.com)

- Jimdo (www.JimdoReview.com)

- Squarespace (www.SquarespaceReview.com)

- Weebly (www.WeeblySiteBuilder.com)

- Homestead (Intuit) (www.HomesteadWebsiteInfo.com)

- Typepad (www.TypepadReview.com)

- Tumblr (www.tumblr.com)

Online Community Platforms

- Ning (www.ning.com)

- SubHub (www.subhub.com)

- SocialGo (www.socialgo.com)

- MemberGate (www.MembergateReview.com)

- Wild Apricot (www.WildApricotReview.com)

Email Publishing and List Management

- AWeber (www.AweberEmailReview.com)

- FeedBlitz (www.FeedblitzReview.com)

- MailChimp (www.mailchimp.com)

Domain Name Registration

- Internet Millionaire Domains (www.InternetMillionaire Domains.com)

- Go Daddy (www.godaddy.com)

Logo Design

- LogoNerds (www.CheapLogoInfo.com)

Text Ads

- AdSense (www.google.com/adsense)
- adBrite (www.adbrite.com)
- Kontera (www.kontera.com)
- Text Link Ads (www.TextLinkAdsReview.com)

Affiliate Program Ads

- Commission Junction (www.cj.com)
- LinkShare (www.LinkshareAffiliateReview.com)
- ShareASale (www.ShareasaleAffiliates.com)
- Site Build It (www.JoinSBI.com)
- Amazon Associates (affiliate-program.amazon.com)
- Click Millionaires Affiliates (www.ClickMillionairesAffiliates.com)

See Chapter 24 for details about these advertising providers and winning strategies for implementing them on your website.

E-commerce Platforms and Shopping Carts

- PayPal (www.PaypalMerchantInfo.com)
- Big Commerce (www.BigCommerceStores.com)
- Yahoo Stores (www.YahooStoreInfo.com)
- Shopify (www.ShopifyStoreInfo.com)

Digital Download Services (These are specialized e-commerce services for the sale of digital downloads as discussed in Chapter 14.)

- ClickBank (www.ClickBankMerchants.com)
- eJunkie (www.ejunkie4downloads.com)
- Payloadz (www.PayloadzReview.com)

CLICK MILLIONAIRES SECRET: The Best Credit Card Processor

There are many online shopping cart services that you can use in conjunction with a traditional credit card merchant account to allow you to accept credit cards online. However, in my experience worrying too much about which credit card processor to use is not worth the time until you have enough revenue for the fees to become significant. (FeeFighters.com is a website that can help you find the best credit card processing services and fee deals if you want to do your own research, though.)

For most new ventures I recommend my favorite online payments service, PayPal, when starting out. PayPal merchant accounts have no up-front cost, require no credit check, and cost only a small percentage of each sale you make. Plus, installing PayPal payment buttons on your site is a simple copy/paste effort that even non-techie entrepreneurs can handle easily.

Outsourcing and Contractor Project Marketplaces

- Elance (www.ElanceOutsourcing.com)
- vWorker (www.vWorkerReview.com)
- oDesk (www.oDeskInfo.com)
- Guru (www.guru.com)
- Freelancer (www.freelancer.com)

Note: Many of the links above and throughout this book are affiliate links. Using them to buy the services recommended won't cost you anything extra (it's an advertising expense paid for by the companies) but may generate an affiliate commission that helps support Click Millionaires charities and programs. Thanks for using them.

The companies I have listed are all reputable and have established track records of reliability. I have used them all myself or at least heard consistently good things about their services. Of course, the Internet marketplace is very dynamic. By the time you read this many of these players may have evolved, merged, or even failed, with new ones and new types of services taking their places. Visit ClickMillionaires.com for the latest information. "Vendor Recommendations" is one of our forum's most popular discussion categories.

easy content publishing strategies

WHETHER YOUR business model relies on product sales or advertising, your new Click Millionaire business must offer interesting or valuable info to attract an audience. Good, original content remains the best way to differentiate your website from the competition. Of course, you can personally write (or podcast or video or whatever) as much content as you'd like. If you base your content on an industry or hobby that you know personally, you can start with almost no research start-up time either. And if you'd like to target an industry that you don't know as much about, you can subscribe to free noozles, blogs, and industry forums online to quickly learn about that industry or target market. (See Chapter 7 for the easy 10-step plan that can quickly position you as an expert.)

Sourcing Content (aka "What Do I Write About?")

Original material is an important differentiator for a new publishing venture, but it also takes a lot of work. The create-your-own-content approach presumes you like to write (or video or podcast) and that your audience also likes what you produce. So to get started I prefer to emphasize *free content*. By "free content" I mean simply quoting, linking to, and/or rewriting content from other professionally produced sites. This a lot less work than trying to create high-quality, original material yourself, especially if you are new to the topic you are targeting or are not a great writer. In fact, many successful e-businesses operate primarily on free content borrowed, linked to, summarized, or repurposed from publicly available sources like blogs and company websites. If your Click Millionaire business has an industry focus, even company press releases can count as valuable news for your audience.

No one has enough time to read everything today, so this simple "filtering" approach where you pick the most relevant news of the day/week/month can be helpful to busy subscribers who don't have time to go searching for the latest news themselves.

Later, after you've proved that there is audience demand in the niche you have targeted, you can write original articles, shoot original videos, record original interviews, or commission your audience's favorite types of content from freelancers.

An Easy Four-Week Content Publishing Plan

Becoming an online publisher can be easier than you think. The attention span of readers online is very short—so your articles or videos don't have to be long or detailed. Most people actually prefer short-form content online (and increasingly on their phones, too). Here's a sample publishing schedule that you can use to publish an interesting, easy-to-produce weekly business-targeted (B2B) blog, noozle, video, or podcast for any interest, industry, or topic:

WEEK 1 CONTENTS

- Headlines from and links to three of the best industry-related articles available online that week.

- Headlines from and links to the two most interesting press releases from industry companies that week.

- One question for the audience asking for their comments and opinions on an industry issue.

- Three updates about industry executives changing jobs.

- A joke.

WEEK 2 CONTENTS

- Headlines from and links to three of the best industry-related articles available online that week.

- Headlines from and links to the two most interesting press releases from industry companies that week.

- The best reader responses to the question you posted the previous week.

- A short article where an industry "expert" answers a question.

- Photos from a recent industry conference (including names and titles of the people pictured).

- A link to a funny YouTube video.

WEEK 3 CONTENTS

‣ Headlines from and links to three of the best industry-related articles available online that week.

‣ Headlines from and links to the two most interesting press releases from industry companies that week.

‣ A review of a recent industry conference from an attendee.

‣ A poll on an industry issue (use free online polling widgets from Vizu.com).

‣ A list of job openings in the industry.

‣ A list of industry executive birthdays in the coming month (including their photos).

WEEK 4 CONTENTS

‣ Headlines from and links to three of the best industry-related articles available online that week.

‣ Headlines from and links to the two most interesting press releases from industry companies that week.

‣ News from Washington: links to articles about recent political developments impacting the industry.

‣ Photos from a recent industry party or charity event (including names and titles of the people pictured).

‣ A trivia question (ideally with a prize for the first, best, or funniest answer).

Get the idea? This kind of industry-insider information is available to your audience, but it is spread all across the Web, hidden in different silos of information. As a Click Millionaire publisher you can profit by packaging it into an easy-to-access, free format. Busy people in any industry love this convenience, especially when you include photos of their most important and attractive executives. If you apply this simple publishing plan to an industry that interests you, I promise that within mere months you will be seen as an industry "expert," even if you have had no prior experience in the field! And that kind of credibility brings the prestige of being a "publisher"—plus advertising dollars and other valuable opportunities like speaking invitations, consulting offers, promotional deals, and more.

Daily Operations

The day-to-day work routine of a Click Millionaire publishing business like this revolves around collecting and publishing information for your audience. Depending on your topic area and the interests of your target market, this likely means surfing the net to read blogs, visiting forums, and connecting with relevant folks via Facebook, Twitter, Google+, or email to collect the latest stories. You can then write up these stories yourself or simply post collections of links to the best items you have found to create your content. Even better—you can hire a freelance editor to do it, creating a Click Millionaire business system that you can grow to make money every day without your personal daily participation.

Of course, the money from this approach is in the follow-up. That may be obvious when speaking about closing sponsorship deals, but you also want to follow up by interacting with your audience, responding to their comments, and encouraging them to share your content online to spread the word about your publication in order to gain additional readers. The more readers you attract, the more viewers (and clickers) there are for your ads, which puts more money in your pocket.

· · · · · · 24 · · · · · ·

the secrets of online advertising

IF YOU'RE reading this book, you're familiar with shopping online. Now it's time to reverse your perspective and start thinking like an online business owner instead of just a shopper: *How do you run a website that makes money from its visitors?*

Selling Products vs. Selling Ads

For e-commerce, it usually goes something like this: You post an offer on a website, a visitor clicks to add your product to your site's "shopping cart," enters his or her credit card info to make a purchase from your site, and shazam! you've made a sale that deposits money in your bank account.

What's a bit more confusing to many folks than this basic e-commerce sales example is how you can make money online from advertising.

How Online Advertising Can Make You Rich

It used to be that you had to have a major audience first before you could sell ads, but not anymore. Today anyone can start a publishing business online and make money by posting ads on their website right from the start. The nickels and dimes of pay-per-click (PPC) ads might not sound like much, but they add up to a great "system" that can help you monetize traffic. I personally make thousands of dollars from PPC ads every month like clockwork, and the money is deposited automatically to my bank.

Online advertising is still the fastest growing sector in the ad world, too. And despite years of double-digit annual growth, the total U.S. spend on internet ads is still just $30 billion annually—that's only a bit more than 15 percent of the total U.S. advertising industry.[1] Globally the digital ad sector is growing at between 15 and 16 percent annually, and it will soon exceed $100 billion in spend annually worldwide.[2]

Think about it. Don't these statistics match your own experience? Hasn't your viewing of Internet ads increased even more than that in recent years? And mobile advertising is about to take off, too. Bottom line: Online advertising still allows profitable new revenue opportunities for you in almost any niche.

How to Find Advertisers and Sponsors

There are four levels of advertising you can use to make money online (see Figure 24–1).

1. *PAY-PER-CLICK (PPC) ADVERTISING.* Best exemplified by Google's pioneering (and dominant) AdSense program, automatically generated PPC ads are the easiest place to start making money from website advertising. Just a free registration and an easy copy-and-paste of ad-serving code into your website will start displaying paying ads on your site. Google's systems (or those of AdSense competitors like adBrite, Word Ads, or others) then review your site's content and keywords to determine what ads are appropriate to show to your visitors. You then get paid every time a visitor clicks on one of the ads. AdSense income alone is enough to keep many Click Millionaire business owners very profitable and happy. Unfortunately, the JavaScript code that is required to run AdSense ads does not work in videos, podcasts, or email messages. (Most Internet service providers and email programs block emails that contain such code because it looks like a virus.) This means that many digital publishers are more dependent on the next three levels of ads.

PPC Click Ads — Affiliate Ads — Custom Sponsorships — Your Product Ads

Easiest
Lowest Value

Most Difficult
Highest Value

Figure 24–1. The Four Types of Ads You Can Profit From Online

2. AFFILIATE PROGRAM ADVERTISING. Copying and pasting into your site the affiliate ad code provided by individual companies displays their ads to your site visitors in a manner similar to PPC ads. However, instead of just a click, affiliate ads usually require the visitor to make a purchase to generate a commission for you. When they do, you'll receive bounties that range from a small percentage of each sale to a large fixed dollar amount, often extending into the hundreds of dollars per sale for high-priced items. This can be very profitable when you find a product that your audience has recurring needs for.

You can pick and choose among thousands of affiliate program offers available through affiliate broker sites like Commission Junction, LinkShare, or ShareASale. You can also apply directly to individual companies to participate in their affiliate programs. Some of the best affiliate programs include:

> **Amazon Associates.** Amazon.com's huge selection, quick delivery, and many free affiliate marketing tools make its affiliate program a great place to start, especially if you are new to affiliate marketing. You're sure to find products that appeal to your audience, but its low commission rates and the unavailability of the program in some states keep it from being my favorite. (affiliate-program.amazon.com/)

> **Site Build It.** A better example is my favorite affiliate program, Site Build It. It can earn you lifetime commissions from marketing SBI's unique combination of website building tools, training, and search engine optimization education, plus a ton of free tools, a helpful forum, and a money-back guarantee. This package is an easy sell to any audience interested in websites or new to e-business. www.JoinSBI.com is my affiliate link for this highly recommended affiliate program.

> **Click Millionaires Affiliate Program.** I invite you to join the Click Millionaires affiliate program, too. You can earn recurring income and help raise money for charity as an affiliate for ClickMillionaires.com and my other products and services. Learn how you can make money helping others build lifestyle businesses for themselves at www.ClickMillionairesAffiliates.com.

Affiliate marketing is always a hot topic in the ClickMillionaires .com Forum, too. Visit to learn about new products that fit your audience, reviews of competing services, and how to increase sales conversions on your affiliate offers.

3. DIRECT ADVERTISING AND CUSTOM SPONSORSHIPS. If you can identify companies that have products appealing to your target market, you can pitch them to sponsor your websites or activities.

Even with a small audience, if your website or services reach a tightly defined and hard-to-reach demographic, there will likely be vendors serving that market who are willing to pay you to reach those readers. For example, almost any industry has specialized insurance companies, conferences, books, travel agents, bankers, lawyers, product suppliers, and even print magazines. Or, a local gym or exercise equipment supplier can be a good sponsor for a personal training website, an insurance company for an online community of daredevils, or a local nursery for a gardening site.

It can be difficult to get companies to pay cash for ads when your readership is still small, so you may want to consider offering free introductory ad packages or bartering when you first get started.

4. YOUR OWN PRODUCTS. As your online business grows you'll find that you develop expertise in your site's topics. That creates the opportunity for you to offer information products of your own to the audience. Ads for *your own* information products are the best because they offer you the highest profit margins. You don't want to spam your own audience but promoting your own products can be highly profitable. You can easily earn $100+ per sale if you create and sell a downloadable product or online service that closely matches your audience's interests. When you do, you'll want to replace some of the generic AdSense, affiliate, or even sponsorship ads with ads for those more profitable products of your own. (Downloadable information products like those discussed in Chapter 14 are great for this.)

The key to making money from online advertising is to choose ads that *match your audience's interests* and serve their needs. The more your ads help your audience, the more likely they are to click and get you paid.

> **CLICK MILLIONAIRES SECRET: Post Your Ads
> Right Away**
> Don't wait until you have a lot of traffic to post your first advertisements. To avoid annoying your audience later, be sure to include ads on your website and in your content from the very start. You want your audience to be used to seeing advertising on your website from the beginning so that they're not surprised when you add it later (which can lead to complaints just when you begin to make money!).

How Much Money Your Website Can Make from Pay-per-Click (PPC) Ads

A "keyword" is a word or short phrase that potential customers are most likely to use to search for your type of info or products online. It's important to determine the keywords most appropriate for your site because it's those keywords that Google uses to decide what ads it shows on your site if you are participating in Google AdSense. For example, if your site's pages are full of references to wicker furniture, Google is going to classify your site under that topic in its search results. If you have installed its PPC ad display code on your site, Google will start serving wicker furniture–related ads on your site.

For a quick estimate of how much your site could make from PPC ads, try writing down a few questions that your target customer might type into Google if searching for solutions like the ones your site will provide. Pull the most important nouns and short phrases out of the simple search questions to find your keywords. For example, here are four simple search queries and their resulting keywords:

- "How do I fix a blender?" Keywords: blender, fix, how to

- "Where can I get cheap airline tickets to Hawaii?" Keywords: Hawaii, tickets, cheap, airline

- "What was the score for last night's Lakers game?" Keywords: Lakers, score, game

› "How can I keep raccoons out of my garden?" Keywords: raccoons, garden

Now these were very simple keyword breakdowns. Professionals get a lot more sophisticated in their keyword analysis, but this should give you the idea.

After you have determined the most likely keywords for your site, visit www.GoogleKeywordsTool.com and click to visit Google's Traffic Estimator tool for some free research. Into the box labeled "Get traffic estimates" type in the keywords that your target customers are likely to use when searching. Click "Estimate" and Google will show you how much advertisers pay for each click received from ads displayed on pages related to that keyword content. Google splits those advertising fees received from pay per click advertisers 51 percent to the publisher (that's you) and keeps 49 percent for itself. So, if your keyword phrase is "Detroit plumber" and AdWords says that advertisers are currently bidding $3.67 for each click from searchers using the phrase "Detroit plumber" in their searches, you'll receive approximately $1.87 for each click on your ads from your site visitors. If your site has 1,000 visitors each month who click on ads triggered by that keyword phrase, you are going to make approximately $1,871 dollars per month by displaying Google's PPC ads that attract those clicks.

Isn't this a pretty amazing research tool and way to make money? And, best of all, it's free!

CLICK MILLIONAIRES SECRET: Kickstarter.com

I'm generally against trying to raise money for your Click Millionaire business because it forces you to give up control of your destiny and distracts you from your business to serve the needs of your investors (who usually have very different goals from you).

But there's a new fund-raising model emerging today: crowdsourcing. For example, Kickstarter.com is an innovative community-based funding

platform that can help you raise financing from people who are as passionate about your niche project as you are. By posting your project on the Kickstarter website you make it available to people worldwide who are looking for creative projects to support.

Although Kickstarter.com started more to fund projects from the worlds of music, film, art, technology, design, food, publishing, and other creative fields, if the core of your new venture or product can be presented as a specific work that needs patronage, you may be able to tap the tens of thousands of people who have already pledged more than $100,000,000 through the site.

To raise money on Kickstarter you set a funding goal ($1,000 or $1,000,000, depending on your project's needs) and a deadline by which it must be funded. If you attract enough donations to reach your goal, the project is funded by charging all the pledgers' credit cards and suddenly you have capital!

I like this crowd-sourced funding model because it helps you build a community of patrons truly interested in your work and you get to keep 100 percent ownership and control over your project.

Here are two quick examples:

- "Detroit Needs a Statue of Robocop!": This project's organizers decided that the 1987 action movie deserved a statue of the title character in my home town where the movie was set. They set a goal of $50,000 and successfully raised $67,436 from almost 3,000 different contributors (including me). The life-sized iron and bronze sculpture is now in production.

- "Pen Type-A: A minimal pen": Brooklyn-based designers Che-Wei Wang and Taylor Levy love pens. They designed a prototype of a high-tech, indestructible, minimalist writing instrument. They posted their project pictures on Kickstarter and asked for help raising $2,500 for further development. They received $281,989!

Of course, not every Kickstarter project explodes like these examples. But the Kickstarter platform offers you another smart way to "find demand first, then build a business"—a proven Click Millionaires success strategy.

CHAPTER 24 NOTES

1. www.businessinsider.com/chart-us-advertising-by-medium-2011-7

2. www.clickz.com/clickz/stats/2092577/digital-attract-percent-global-spend-2011

PART SEVEN

LIFESTYLE LESSONS FROM CLICK MILLIONAIRE INTERNET ENTREPRENEURS

25

how to choose the best lifestyle business system for you

WHAT IF YOU had thousands of fans worldwide looking to you for guidance, information, expertise, or inspiration? How about thousands of paying customers for your services or products waiting for you to wake up each day? That may sound out of reach, but you truly do have the opportunity to get there from where you are today.

Now, here's the big question: What would you be doing for these fans and customers? Some of the paths we have now discussed include building lifestyle businesses by:

▸ Serving the information or community needs of people who share your niche interests.

‣ Transferring specialized knowledge from your job or learning new skills to position yourself as an expert.

‣ Creating new downloadable information products.

‣ Promoting, reviewing, aggregating, and filtering the products and information produced by other companies.

‣ Freelancing (or at least virtual assistant-ing) to make money, learn new skills, and maybe even reinvent yourself.

The Click Millionaires road map differs for each person. I have seen solopreneurs have the best luck at doing the tasks they like and are good at, while outsourcing the rest. I know that may sound simplistic, but that's the bottom line: Do what you like and enjoy and are good at (assuming it has some commercial value, of course) and you will enjoy what you're doing, you'll do it well, and you'll keep on doing it. Outsource the tasks you don't like, because trying to make money doing work you don't enjoy, don't understand, or aren't qualified for will likely lead to discouragement and failure (especially if you also have competing obligations and limited time due to a family, children, etc.). It may sound self-indulgent to focus on the tasks you like, but if you don't, you are just creating another job you dislike. And I'm sure we agree that that is not the goal here!

The Click Millionaires Business System Checklist

Here's a checklist of factors for you to consider when evaluating the many new business ideas that are hopefully now percolating in your head and in your Click Millionaires Idea Journal. Very few ideas will pass all these tests. But those that do will be laptop lifestyle businesses worth pursuing. Rank your business ideas for each of these components using the 1 (low)–5 (high) scale provided.

CLICK MILLIONAIRES NEW BUSINESS SYSTEM EVALUATION CHECKLIST	☹ 1	2	3	4	☺ 5
My Lifestyle					
My personal interest in the niche					
Production activities interest me (writing, talking, video, social media, etc.)					
At least three items from your Lifestyle Design Shopping List (e.g., work from home, make own hours, etc.)					
1.					
2.					
3.					
Market					
Audience need					
Niche size—not too big, but not too small					
Low competition					
Marketing angle					
Revenue Opportunities					
Money being spent by users or advertisers					
High-paying PPC or affiliate ads available					
Profitable products available for sale or promotion					
Recurrence and upsell potential					
Operations					
Fast and easy to start up					
Inexpensive to start up					

	1	2	3	4	5
Low costs of daily production and operations					
Few technological skills required					
Technology required					
Costs of production and operations					
Strategy					
Scalability					
Favorable trends and growth potential					
Gut check—Will this create satisfying and profitable work I can be proud of?					
Column Totals:					
ALL COLUMNS TOTAL:					

How to Use and Score this Checklist: Create a separate sheet for each of your best business concepts. Rank each business system idea you have on a scale of 1 (low) to 5 (high) for each of the categories. Add up the scores from all columns together to create a new business opportunity score for each idea you're considering.

Here's what the scores can tell you:

  1–35 Not Likely

36–45 Needs Work

46–60 Possible

61–75 Interesting and Worth More Research

76–90 Very Promising

  90+ *Aha!*

You'll be able to evaluate multiple business ideas faster using this checklist. It includes the Click Millionaires Lifestyle Business Design

Success Principles and other decision factors I use personally when deciding whether or not to invest my time in a new business. Ideas scoring low are not going to work, while a high score could be the Click Millionaire lifestyle business system you're seeking.

If you make copies, you can use this checklist repeatedly to evaluate your different new ideas and it will make it easier to compare competing ideas, too.

You can also download a free, expanded version of this checklist after you sign up for the free emails from ClickMillionaires.com. With more than 30 factors for you to evaluate and rank, it can help ensure you are investing your valuable time for maximum return.

26

the 10-step action plan for redesigning your life starting today

IT'S EASY TO feel overwhelmed by all the new information and new opportunities you could pursue. To consolidate all the information this book has given you so far, it's time for an action plan to help you move forward. Here are 10 steps that you can take to start building your Click Millionaire lifestyle business today.

STEP 1: REALLOCATE YOUR TIME

Look at your daily schedule and determine how much time you can commit to investing in a new venture. Take whatever you can get, but try to commit a consistent number of hours each week toward the many small steps you'll need to get going. Force yourself to turn off the TV and do something constructive repeatedly. The sooner you start building your new pursuit into your lifestyle the better. Even one hour a week can add up over time, and one hour a day is even better.

STEP 2: REDESIGN YOUR SCHEDULE

Think hard about where you can find more time to invest in pursuit of your new lifestyle. For example, save some vacation days for research and planning, ask your boss for a schedule change that allows you to work from home or avoid the worst commuting hours. Maybe even change some of your responsibilities to project-based (results) instead of hours-based (face time) to free up time that you can invest in your new business.

STEP 3: START A BUDGET

Divert whatever money you can afford into a new savings account. (I like free online ones like those available from INGDirect.com.) Set up an automatic weekly or monthly transfer of whatever you can afford into this account to start building a nest egg. Set this money aside specifically for new business research, training, and development expenses. Even if you don't know what you're going to do or when, start saving now so you have capital to implement or even quit your job later. Even $10 a week can add up over time.

Note: You can do these first three steps without even knowing what your new lifestyle business is going to be! Start reorganizing your life around what you want it to become and your lifestyle will start to change to reflect your lifestyle goals.

STEP 4: ANALYZE YOUR LIFESTYLE GOALS

Revisit the Lifestyle Design Shopping List from Chapter 4. Work through the exercises there to help identify what is most important to you. Don't skimp on this part—if you don't know where you want to go it's hard to get there! Extra time spent on strategic thinking is a good investment.

STEP 5: GENERATE BUSINESS IDEAS

By now I hope you have put to good use the many earlier exercises to generate ideas for starting a new online lifestyle business of your own. If not, then now is the time to revisit the steps of the Click Millionaires Method for Business Niche Identification (Chapter 20), and get busy filling the pages of your Click Millionaires Idea Journal. Combining the several filters of what you like, what you can deliver cost-effectively, how to market it competitively, and the Click Millionaires Lifestyle Business Design Success Principles will help you narrow down even the wildest ideas to practical businesses. So go ahead—dream big and have fun thinking up clever ways to reinvent your life.

STEP 6: DO SOME RESEARCH

Educating yourself about the field you have chosen and your competition is a good investment of time, too.

- *Read books.* Read three to five books. Half of these books should be about your chosen topic areas and target markets to help you become an expert. The other half of them should be about "how to do it" online by building websites, Internet marketing, and product development and differentiation. Then stop reading! That's enough. *Money comes from doing, not reading.*

- *Go online.* Set up free Google Alerts to automatically email you the latest blog posts and web page updates on the topics that you're exploring. Look for holes in the market and ways that you can serve the needs of people you would enjoy working with.

› *Study your competitors.* Subscribe to the noozles or blogs, buy the products of, or join the communities of three competitors to learn what they're doing and identify ways that you could improve on it.

Note: Avoid "Analysis Paralysis": Don't overdo the research! Research is often used as a crutch to avoid the fear of failure. Set a time line that allows you to learn enough to be dangerous and then a deadline for moving forward.

STEP 7: DON'T SPEND MONEY

We are all trained to think that buying stuff will help solve our problems. But if you're going to create something new and valuable, it's more likely to come from inside you than from the latest "guru" product or course. Don't spend more than you can afford on a highly promoted business, marketing, or product development course. Instead, spend at least 30 days just looking, reading, researching the competition, discussing with friends, and thinking about what you could and should do online. (Of course spending a little money to educate yourself, learn about the competition, and participating in forums and blogs and social networks is okay and better than just reading but only *if* you can afford it and *if* those activities are advancing your project rather than just distracting you.)

STEP 8: START A TEST SITE

Once you have an idea of the direction you'd like to go, start a test website. When you're getting started, you'll probably find this much harder than you expected. However, you'll see that building websites is like learning a language. At first it all seems like difficult gibberish but with repeated exposure and practice, you'll soon learn words, then phrases, and soon be able to build your own sites faster and faster. There's no need to learn any programming these days to build a basic website. For this experimental phase, I recommend using a cheap or free website building service like Weebly, Blogger, or WordPress. Of course, you can hire outsourced contractors to help you, too.

And, if your business is more about podcasting or videos or auctions, then you'll want to invest this time learning how to use BlogTalkRadio.com, YouTube, or eBay instead.

Note: Your test site does not have to be perfect, it doesn't even need to be good. You don't have to put your real name on it or tell all your friends about it, either. Your goal is simply to get some hands-on experience of how e-business works. It's better to do that privately, when there's little money on the table. You are going to make mistakes and are going to look stupid at least once, so the sooner you quietly get past that part the better!

STEP 9: TAKE ODD JOBS

If you are trying to change careers or learn new skills, try doing some freelance contracting on the side, away from your current job. Join project marketplaces like Elance or oDesk to see what skills employers are seeking. You can even surf the "Gigs" section on your local CraigsList to see what small projects you can take on to get paid while learning. Even if you don't make much, getting paid to learn valuable new skills is a great deal.

STEP 10: ESTABLISH YOUR BRANDING

Start brainstorming domain names once you have an idea of the business direction you are headed. You want a name that is short, easy to spell and remember, and available, ideally with a ".com" extension. There are not many of those left, so this can be harder than it sounds.

(Domain name brainstorming is a popular topic in the Click Millionaires Forum, so drop by if you'd like the community's help with this.)

Once you have a good domain name, be sure to join the more popular social networking services using your new brand as your username. You want to establish your usernames with these services to make it easy for customers to find you (and to make sure competitors don't take them).

‣ ‣ ‣

Following this low-cost 10-Step Action Plan can get you on your way to building a successful Click Millionaire lifestyle business of your own. I hope that it's helpful to you in changing your life for the better.

27

conclusion
winning click millionaires
success strategies

There is only one success—to be able to spend your life in your own way.
—Christopher Morley, US author and journalist

WHAT HAVE YOU done in your life that you love so much you enjoy sharing it with others? Today you have better opportunities than ever before to turn that interest into a business that pays you to do the work you were born to do. You get to choose the USP— unique service and purpose—that powers your new business and lifestyle so that you can find success on your own terms.

Here are a few more strategic thoughts to help inspire you and set your mindset in the proper, positive direction before you stop reading and start doing.

Transition Strategies to Help You Upgrade Your Life

Starting your own business may sound like a big, scary challenge but it's easier and cheaper than ever. You can reach wider markets than ever before even if you're not an expert in the technologies that make the Internet work. Even small ideas can grow into major revenue generators given the right timing (now!) and wide enough market reach (worldwide!). As this book's many examples have shown, the technology, costs, and even the fears of wasting your time or failure can all be managed today with the proper plan and coaching. There's no better time than now to seize the reins of your life and make your mark.

Get your e-business started now on a part-time basis, instead of quitting your job to go whole hog. Slow and steady can win this race. After-hours, weekends, bits and pieces of progress stitched together over months, even years, can grow to the payoff you're seeking: $5 the first month, $50 each month a few months later, $500 a month after that, eventually growing to $1,000, $5,000, or $50,000 per month. How does that sound? This slower approach can also give you time to test different approaches and products, time to react to competitors, and time to develop the relationships with customers and partners that will pay off over time.

Overcoming Your Past

Everything in your past has succeeded in bringing you here today. You may have had disappointments in the past but today is a new day for you. Most of us operate on assumptions that were programmed into us when we were small. And our expectations have been conditioned by the supposed "overnight successes" that the TV and Internet bombard us with. This can lead to frustration, insecurity, and even a sense of failure. Instead of settling for less than you hoped out of life, I'd like to see you upgrade your attitude, lifestyle, and achievement mindset. How about increasing your expectations for success instead? More positive expectations today can lead to more self-confidence, which leads to further progress toward success.

A small success online today can generate more income for you and upgrade your expertise and self-confidence, too. It can also be built upon for more success tomorrow. Grow that business system (or start another) and you'll be on your way to working less and living more. And every year that you are more successful in designing your lifestyle to achieve the success you seek, the more that success will *compound* itself to create more success in your life.

Overcoming Greed

Those "get rich quick" moneymaking strategies promoted online and in TV infomercials are as silly as they sound. Click Millionaires are realistic about the facts—it takes real time, real effort, and even some luck to really "make it" in any kind of business.

Click Millionaires reject the common view that accumulation of wealth is the best use of our time, recognizing instead that money is just helpful gasoline for life's journey, not the destination. While you need "enough" money to survive and thrive, money alone won't improve your mental approach to life. It's better to reorganize your life to be happy now because more money will simply exaggerate your current condition. Retirement is also not necessarily a goal of Click Millionaires. No matter how old you are, satisfying work is an important part of happiness. Why would you quit working if you are enjoying yourself and helping others, too?

Don't Hold Your Breath Waiting for Approval

Back at the beginning of this book we talked about permission. As an employee you need to ask for permission to do anything non-routine. You need permission from your boss to come in late, take a day off, start or finish a project, etc. I asked you then to imagine what could happen if you stopped asking for permission and instead began to redesign your life based on your own creativity, moving toward a more flexible and lucrative future. As you have since seen throughout this book, one of the beauties of the Click Millionaires lifestyle design approach is that you can build yourself a new lifestyle where *you don't need permission to be yourself anymore.*

There is a deeper issue here, too: approval. We all seek approval from others. In business it's mostly your boss's approval that is important but the approval of coworkers, subordinates, and customers is important, too. You also need the approval of your friends, family, and spouse if you are going to feel good about yourself. Unfortunately approval is hard to come by as a solopreneur. As a Click Millionaire there is no longer a boss for you to impress and your family may not even understand what you are doing online!

You'll need to develop enough confidence in your own ideas that you pursue them even without a boss looking over your shoulder. This revolution in self-confidence can improve your life even more than money. Self-esteem is earned, not bought, and it pays dividends every single day. Get going online and you'll soon find it liberating to be able to focus on topics you like and be truly productive instead of wasting time trying to impress coworkers or please the boss.

Finding Support Online

Change can scare people. You may even need to find new friends who can be supportive of you in your new endeavors. Where to look? Online of course! Try social networks and forums for your chosen topic or industry, Meetup.com, Facebook, Twitter, Google+, the ClickMillionaires.com Forum, etc. They call it "social" media because it's a great way to meet people. You need and deserve a support group, especially if you're new to online business. There are friendly folks from around the world online right now who share your interests in self-improvement and entrepreneurship. They would be happy to help you with whatever is keeping you from upgrading your lifestyle. Becoming a part of these communities can accelerate your success.

Failure *Is* an Option

If plan A fails, remember you have 25 letters left.
                                        —Chris Guillebeau, U.S. blogger and author

You don't hear this message much, but don't be afraid to *stop*. The odds of you getting it exactly right with your first Internet business venture are quite small. So what? What's your downside anyway?

Picking a business model is like choosing a major in college— you're likely to change it anyway. You'll probably be like I was—I started out pre-med but that changed as soon as I took chemistry! I found plenty of success on alternate paths that I didn't even know existed when I began.

If you don't see potential first from your market research, and especially later from the testing techniques outlined in Chapter 21, then quit! You may have lost some time and a little money. But imagine what you can learn! And imagine how that learning will enhance your future efforts, too. You've got to try if you're going to succeed— and it's okay to adjust course along the way. I would rather see you fail 10 times quickly and cheaply than painfully dragging out a single failure over months or years and thousands of dollars.

Don't let your ego get in the way. Protect your wallet and stop before you waste too much time and money. Internet businesses are low-cost to start, so there's nothing keeping you from simply starting over. As discussed in Chapter 26, give yourself a budget for both time and money to explore your lifestyle design ideas and try them out. Use the cushion of the income from your job to experiment for a while. Don't go crazy and mortgage your house to invest everything in the first idea you run across. Decide what you can afford to lose and (if necessary) call that amount of time and money an investment in your future so you can move on. Just be sure that you profit from your ventures by *learning from them* even if they don't succeed (or especially when they don't!). The sooner you stop, the sooner you can start over by *reinvesting* your new knowledge or skills into a new venture instead.

Think Projects, Not Company

Structure your projects so that failure is not fatal.
—Seth Godin, U.S. marketing and management author

Working for a company means putting all of your eggs in one basket. But a new way of thinking about careers has been pioneered in Hollywood, and it's seen increasingly in Silicon Valley, too. Hollywood films, TV shows, and music have long employed people on a project basis rather than as full-time jobs. You can work that way today by using the same skills applied multiple times to different ventures. Whether the projects are your own or for someone else, either way you make money and learn more skills to apply next time. Over time you can get better and better but even if a few projects fail along the way, you're still progressing.

Back yourself up with staff that does anything you don't know how to do or don't want to do. You can find the information or support or people you need for almost anything online—it's all out there if you look. When you're ready you can step up to run (and own) your own projects and turn them into Click Millionaire lifestyle businesses. Start new websites and then hand them off to cheaper help so you can get on with the next one! Succeed a few times and you may find yourself like me—with a team of great people I can call on for specific skills whenever I start a new website business. And that allows for repeat performances as they help me build new projects into additional lifestyle businesses for my portfolio of profitable Click Millionaire business systems.

Don't Believe the Hype—Avoid Time- and Money-Wasting "Gurus"

Don't think a guru is going to help you more than a customer.
—Dan Andrews, TropicalMBA.com

As you pursue your new interest in lifestyle design, you're going to be on the hunt for answers. It's natural to look for the most efficient ways to accelerate your success. But don't expect to find the answers to the big questions from someone else. You'll run into many "experts" and "gurus" online with exciting offers that sound like easy money. And some of them have even actually made money online. But that's often because of hype about their new product launches rather than because their advice or products are so valuable. What you need is not an "exclusive new video course" or an "executive platinum guru weekend retreat package." You need personalized advice specific to your lifestyle business idea and personal situation.

With this book I've tried hard to give you a process to follow that will help you develop that plan for yourself cost-effectively and help you make the best decisions specifically for you. As soon as you're ready for more, get together with friends, join a support group (online or off), or just come join ClickMillionaires.com—that's why I started it, precisely to help entrepreneurs like you get the support and answers they need!

Even better? Launch a website and try to sell some stuff. Real feedback from real customers will teach you more than any guru's advice.

Avoid the Envy Machine

Once you're online, beware of what Gina Trapani of the Lifehacker blog calls the "envy machine." By participating in the blogosphere and social media, you're participating in social circles populated by not only your family, friends, and audience, but also mentors, competitors, and even celebrities. Be careful about taking it all too seriously or comparing yourself to others. It may seem like many of those folks are outperforming you, but you can't see behind the scenes. Many of them have been working hard for years before you even started. Others are supported by larger companies, previous experience, family money, personal connections, or other advantages that you probably can't replicate.

Social media is not real life. It's more like a high school reunion where everyone carefully chooses what to highlight. And, surprise, surprise, they tend to magnify the good stuff! You might feel bad if you have competitors (or even friends) who have large audiences. But that comparison is not productive, and it's not fair to you either. With the wide reach of the Internet you are *always* going to be just a few clicks away from people more successful than you are. If that was a problem in the real world, it's only been magnified online. But envying your competitor's 100,000 email subscribers, 10,000 Facebook friends or 100,000 followers on Google+ isn't going to improve your daily life as much as continued positive focus toward your own lifestyle redesign goals.

Part of your reason for building your Click Millionaire business (and reading this book) is to begin charting your own course. You've chosen to *set your own standards* for success so don't waste your time worrying about how your progress compares to others online. You are on this path because you have a commitment to developing your own vision, to building a business with integrity that rewards you for your hard work and that helps you build a meaningful life for those you care most about. Don't fuel the envy machine and you'll be on your way to success on your own terms, a true Click Millionaire.

Helping People Never Goes Out of Style

We make a living by what we get. But we make a life by what we give.
— Winston Churchill, British prime minister and statesman

The specifics of how to find success on the Internet change constantly, and often unpredictably. So I've tried to guide you away from building your business based on a certain kind of marketing or some traffic attraction "trick" that you learn online. Instead you need to identify real customer needs and help people. No matter which new online marketing strategy is in style, or what changes Google or Facebook or Amazon force onto the marketplace, or what new laws or taxes or privacy regimes emerge to complicate online commerce, helping other people will always be a good foundation on which to build your business. Even if your favorite marketing tactic or product strategy suddenly becomes outmoded, if you are solving problems for people and improving their lives, they will become repeat customers and tell their friends, too.

Business Can Be a Way to Express Your Life's Purpose

I see two ways you can go through life. The first is to assume the universe is mechanical, and you are simply a cog in a giant machine. You are playing a role dictated merely by circumstances and biology. This is a credible path accepted by billions.

An alternative is to hope and believe that your existence is more than that—that your existence, in fact, represents a unique opportunity for you to influence the world. You are here, and you have abilities and potential that go far beyond simply eating, sleeping, and procreation. Your self-awareness and capacity for creativity, strategic planning, self-improvement, and compassion have created you as a one-in-trillions opportunity to become something greater. So the second way that you can go through life is to see that your life's mission is to use your power for good. Who do you want to be? How can you improve yourself and the lives of those you care about? How can you make a difference?

Business is usually treated as somehow separate from "who we really are" but I think that's silly, especially when you consider how much time most of us spend at work these days! Instead entrepreneurship is a huge personal growth opportunity for you and online business offers you a platform to do more than just make a living. It can help you share your Unique Service and Purpose with the world. You want more, you deserve more, you have the capacity to offer more, and now you have the tools to be able to do more, too.

All that's left is the will to do it. How about starting now?

Take Action Today

Many people fail at making money online and at taking charge of their own lives. But I know that it's possible even for you because I do it myself every day. The struggle to find success for yourself is not easy or quick but I hope that this book has helped you see your way forward to restructuring your life so that you can greet every day with enthusiasm.

You can find a thousand reasons and excuses for waiting to take action until x, y, or z "changes" in your life. But why wait? Why put your fate in the hands of people, bosses, and circumstances outside your control? If you hope to get results, why not get started changing your life *now*? Especially if the actions are small, the sooner you get going, the sooner they will add up to change the circumstances for you.

Your Life—A Limited Time Offer

Your life is a limited time offer that only *you* can redeem. You can redesign your day-to-day life to live more the way you want—you can change your life and career in that direction by following the guidance in this book. It won't necessarily make you a millionaire but it will help you live more like one every day. Choose the world you live in by identifying what you most want to change about your life and head that way!

What's Next?

Reading is great but doing is better. Would you like to continue the career and lifestyle redesign process you have started here? Whether you're a new entrepreneur who doesn't even have a website yet, a small business looking attract more customers, or a major corporation seeking strategy guidance to compete better online, we can help you at ClickMillionaires.com. Membership in the Click Millionaires Forum is *free* for you as a purchaser of this book at ClickMillionaires Reader.com.

ClickMillionaires.com is also your source for more personalized business and online marketing advice, Private Coaching Calls with me, helpful mastermind teams, and my strategic consulting work and speaking services.

I look forward to hearing from you soon. Please come join us to start making a difference in your own life—and in the lives of others, too.

Let's make it happen!

Scott Fox

epilogue
click millionaires
reinvestment strategies

WHAT TO DO when you succeed as a Click Millionaire? Gradually you start finding you have more free time. It's subtle at first but one day you find yourself out for lunch on a typical Tuesday and you don't need to rush back. Or your kid's school or your church needs a hand on a Friday morning and you find that you can go. And when you walk away from your desk for those "slacker" activities, you find that your bank account keeps growing—even with less work from you!

Woo hoo! Your Click Millionaire business system is working and every aspect of your life and future begins to benefit.

The Click Millionaires Business System Success Cycle

Once you find your free time (and wallet) growing, you'll face happy decisions about what to do with your extra time and money. There are two directions I'd point you in:

- Reinvesting your free time toward achieving more of your own lifestyle goals and creating more profitable businesses. Once you've made your first few dollars online, there's no reason that you can't do it again. And then again and again. If you build the Click Millionaires Lifestyle Business Design Success Principles into your business models, your new ventures should scale and generate recurring income repeatedly. Then you can start working less and living more, and even *giving back*.

- Reinvesting in your community by helping others. Giving back is a key part of how I define success as a Click Millionaire. *Will you join me?* You may not yet have all you want, but if you're reading this, you are far better off than billions of others on the planet right now. "Reinvesting" some of your success in your own life and the lives of those around you feels good and helps make the world a better place, too.

The Click Millionaires Reinvestment Program

If you agree with the lifestyle design approach I've shared in this book, I hope that you'll join me in what I call the "Click Millionaires Reinvestment Program." Even if today you have little money to spare, or technical expertise, as a Click Millionaire you still have lots to offer others. The most dedicated members at ClickMillionaires .com aim to contribute at least 10 percent to others every month right from the start of their lifestyle redesign process. (I borrowed this concept from churches because I wanted to formalize the commitment to others in my own life.)

This is 10 percent of your time, your money, your prayers—whatever works for you as a way to live generously. And you can define "community" in whatever way works for you, too. It may be helping someone in your neighborhood, the people in your office, your family, new members of the ClickMillionaires.com community, or a deserving charity. No one is keeping score except you, but we Click Millionaires define "success" as including *service to others* as part of our daily lives. I lead this strategy myself by donating the profits from my books to charity to help underprivileged kids like I used to be.

Examples of easy activities that you can pursue to reinvest in your community are under discussion all the time in the Click Millionaires Forum. I hope that you'll join these discussions. We would like to help you build a lifestyle business that you can be proud of and help you share your success to help others, too.

Would You Like Your Business Featured?

If you're living a Click Millionaire lifestyle, let's work together to promote your business and inspire others to greater success, too!

I'm always looking for small business success stories to feature on my Click Millionaires Success Show podcasts and in my books. If your business model, marketing, or niche is interesting and can help demonstrate the principles of lifestyle business success to other aspiring entrepreneurs, send me an email. All submissions to "stories@clickmillionaires.com" are reviewed carefully. I'm looking for stories that demonstrate clever Internet marketing or product development, and it helps if they are fun, funny, or unusual, too.

Looking for a Profitable Online Business?

If you're excited about Internet business but not sure where to start, learn how you can make money for yourself and help support Click Millionaires programs and charities at www.ClickMillionairesAffiliates.com. Help me help others by sharing your expertise and getting involved today.

ACKNOWLEDGMENTS

There's a wave of new opportunity rippling through modern society. It offers huge potential for both business and personal development but only some are smart enough to take action to profit from it. By reading this book you have shown that you are one of these clever few, the Click Millionaires. My crusade to help improve lives through Internet entrepreneurship started with *Internet Riches*, continued with *e-Riches 2.0*, and already you're here reading my third book! Thanks so much to you and all my readers worldwide who have supported this mission—and thank you for reading this book. I hope that my work helps you realize more of your personal potential to succeed, both financially and personally, and that it is helpful to you in creating the lifestyle you want and deserve.

All business, demographic, and technological trends point toward lifestyle businesses as the wave of the future. People don't just want to make more money, they want to realize their personal potential and live better lives. Luckily readers like you, my agents Lacy Lynch, Shannon Marven, and Jan Miller, and my friends at the American Management Association (my publisher), continue to agree with this.

Thanks to my AMACOM team including Bob Nirkind, Barry Richardson, Hank Kennedy, Jenny Wesselmann, Rosemary Carlough, Irene Majuk, Jim Bessent, Kama Timbrell, Debbie

Posner, Therese Mausser, Cathleen Ouderkirk, Nate Ouderkirk, William Helms, Andy Ambraziejus, and the entire sales and publicity teams, plus Terry Wybel and the team at Continental Sales.

My sincere thanks also go out to the Click Millionaires profiled in the book especially Connie Mettler, Dave Powers, Kristin Espinasse, Fabio Rosati, Al Peterson, Randy Cassingham, Betty Thesky, Beau Blackwell, Rob Ludlow, Ann Sieg, Amit Agarwal, Manny Hernandez, Wayne Hurlbert, Andrew Warner, Khrystyne Robillard-Smith, Kristof Lindner, Giancarlo Massaro, Tawnya Sutherland, Jason Sadler, Lisa Hendey, Matt Rodriguez, and to the folks who facilitated the interviews including Jason Rosenthal, Christina Lee, Keith Do, Carrie Stuart, and Heather Sharp.

Speaking of Click Millionaires, thanks also to my Featured Member Award winners and friends from ClickMillionaires.com, especially Judith, Marie, Tony, Eva, Kat, Melinda, The Musselwhites, Nate, Sandra, Cy, Sonya, Dave, Liz, Dina, Patrick, Richard, Jeremy, Jane, Hector, Steven, Ivette, Diana, Noah, Seth, Linda, Walter, Krum, and Michael.

Thanks for guidance and inspiration to Seth Godin, Robert Kiyosaki, Bill O'Reilly, Tim Ferriss, David Bach, Darren Hardy, Tim Sanders, Anthony Robbins, Thomas J. Stanley, T. Harv Eker, Michael Ellsberg, Ramit Sethi, Guy Kawasaki, Chris Brogan, Ken Evoy, Bob Lefsetz, Chris Guerriero, Makeda Wubneh, Ron Will, Jacki Bilsborrow, Barb Ford, Chuck Greenwood, Lou Fabale, Michael Whalen, and Sully, Russ, and Maureen from *The Big Biz Show*.

Thanks also to the Ritz-Carlton Laguna Niguel for hospitality, to Panera for plenty of writing fuel, and to Fitdesk. And, most importantly of all, thanks to the beautiful family that inspires my work daily and keeps me striving for even more free time to spend with them—Katherine and the girls, my mom, Ti-Ta and Shung-Jong, Jonathan, and Carie.

All my best for your success.

ABOUT THE AUTHOR

I used to hate my job like you do. But after I figured out that anyone can build their own business on the Internet today, I graduated from "working for the man" to making money online on my own terms. Today I'm a Click Millionaire who works part-time, on projects I enjoy, and with no boss (except my lovely wife and kids, of course). Now I run my family's online businesses, coach lifestyle entrepreneurs worldwide from my home in beautiful southern California, and I donate the profits from my books to charity.

After graduating from the University of Michigan and Stanford Law School, I earned my e-commerce and online marketing expertise by building successful businesses online. These range from niche startups and websites for TV celebrities like Bill O'Reilly and Larry King, to the multibillion dollar online division of a Fortune 500 corporation, to my own ClickMillionaires.com, the friendliest lifestyle entrepreneur success coaching community online.

My mission is to help entrepreneurs and small business owners like you learn to profit from the Internet "lifestyle business" revolution. I hope my books, blog, podcasts, and ClickMillionaires.com Success Forum help you redesign your career and upgrade your life, too.